# Nahaliel The Valley of God

# Nahaliel The Valley of God

## The IDEAL journey of the Believer

**KEITH IRICK**

XULON PRESS ELITE

Xulon Press Elite
2301 Lucien Way #415
Maitland, FL 32751
407.339.4217
www.xulonpress.com

© 2019 by Keith Irick

All rights reserved solely by the author. The author guarantees all contents are original and do not infringe upon the legal rights of any other person or work. No part of this book may be reproduced in any form without the permission of the author. The views expressed in this book are not necessarily those of the publisher.

Unless otherwise indicated, Scripture quotations taken from the King James Version (KJV)–*public domain*.

Printed in the United States of America.

ISBN-13: 978-1-5456-7304-1

INTRODUCTION

# Salvation – The Starting Point for Every Believer

Jesus told Nicodemus in John chapter 3, "*You must be born again*". Nicodemus was a *religious* leader. The definition of *religion* is simply, "believing in a higher power than yourself." If he had to accept Jesus as Lord, then obviously, religion can't save you. In His famous, oft quoted conversation with Nicodemus, Jesus went on to say, "*For God so loved the world that He gave His only Begotten Son, that whosoever believeth in Him should not perish, but have everlasting life.*" (John 3:16) Religion can't save you; a relationship with Jesus can. Isaiah 43:11 says "*I, even I, am the Lord; and besides Me there is no savior.*" (KJV used throughout unless otherwise noted)

The Bible teaches us that "works" won't gain you acceptance into heaven either. "*For by grace are you saved through faith; and that not of yourselves: it is the gift of God: not of works, lest any man should boast*" (Ephesians 2:8, 9). Works are a natural byproduct of true salvation, but working to obtain salvation is not a possibility. Jesus is "*the Way, the Truth, and the Life.*" If you want eternal *Life,* (salvation,) you must know the *Truth*, and He will show you the *Way*. Jesus has already done the work for us; our part is to receive His act of grace by faith.

Regardless of your chronological age at the time you accepted Jesus as your Savior, you are a babe in Christ. Babies need care; feeding, clothing, burping, and holding. God doesn't want us to remain in this infant state. He wants us to learn to feed ourselves on His word; to clothe ourselves in His righteousness; to utilize the body the way it was designed; and finally, to edify others while becoming less selfish and self-centered.

The purpose of this book is to equip you with tools that enable you to progress in the Christian walk. Salvation is the starting point, not the goal. Jesus instructed His followers to make disciples, not converts. Obviously avoiding hell is a blessing for all eternity, but personal fire insurance is not going to benefit others. We must mature so that we can disciple others and reflect Biblical principles in order to attract the lost towards Jesus.

What is maturity? How do you define it, and what does it look like? As defined by Webster, to be mature is "having completed natural growth and development; having attained a final or desired state; or a characteristic of or suitable to a mature individual." Teleios, the Greek word for maturity is used 19 times in the New Testament. A teleios Christian, according to the Word of God, is an individual that promotes unity of the faith, gives all he has and is to the Lord, and is constantly meditating on the Word of God. Hebrews 5;13,14 explains maturity this way, *"13 For every one that useth milk is unskilful in the word of righteousness: for he is a babe. 14 But strong meat belongeth to them that are of full age, even those who by reason of use have their senses exercised to discern both good and evil."* I underlined the word "use" in this scripture to emphasize the importance of using what you

*For Every Believer*

know. The Bible is the moral compass that points towards a mature lifestyle, Jesus like attributes. An unselfish lifestyle that makes a positive impact for the Kingdom of God. But it is your responsibility to stay on course, apply what you learn from the Word.

When you asked Jesus into your life you said goodbye to the world, its ways, and its values. You began a journey, not to Heaven but to maturity. The place where you can be used, be fruitful, and fulfill the vision God has for you. You cannot disciple others if you are still on the bottle, a baby Christian. 2 Peter 1 describes the mature Christian as faithful, virtuous, knowledgeable, temperate, patient, godly, and charitable. Are you there yet? Me either, but at least we have left on the journey. Let's say goodbye to the world system and its ways. Let's dare to believe what God says and thinks about us. Let's accomplish what He desires for our life. Let's grow up.

Israel began its journey by leaving Egypt, (a type of the world) to a better place. Israel's destination was Canaan, a land flowing with milk and honey, (prosperity); a place of rest, where God would protect them and bless them physically, spiritually, and economically. God is still calling man out of Egypt and into His rest, *"Come all ye that labor and are heavy laden and I will give you rest."* Entering that rest isn't easy, it's a process. We must grow in faith through the knowledge of Jesus Christ and by a relationship with Him. Good relationships take time to develop. You may not be where you know you should be at this time, but take heart; you're not where you used to be. A friend of mine likes to express it this way, "I haven't arrived yet, but thank God, I have left." Like my friend you are on your way. The length of the journey will be largely dependent upon your desire to cultivate your relationship with the Creator.

*Nahaliel The Valley of God*

Sadly, like so many of our testimonies could bear out, what should have been an eleven-day trip for Israel turned into forty years. Why? They didn't have the proper "valley mentality." They murmured and complained like babies continuously. This attitude came to a head in Numbers 21. Look at verses 5 – 9. *"And the people spake against God, and against Moses. Wherefore have ye brought us up out of Egypt to die in the wilderness? For there is no bread, neither is there any water; and our soul loatheth this light bread. And the Lord sent fiery serpents among the people and they bit the people; and much people of Israel died. Therefore, the people came to Moses and said, we have sinned, for we have spoken against the Lord, and against thee; pray unto the Lord that He take away the serpents from us. And Moses prayed for the people."*

> **"The valleys reveal to us what we need deliverance from. We in turn rely upon the Holy Spirit to direct us in walking it out."**

Before you get too critical of the Israelites, put yourself in their shoes. We haven't changed much since then. We want everything to be easy. We have drive-thrus for all occasions, from fast food to fast marriages. The devil has fed us the lie that if it isn't easy it can't be God. Or, if I'm going through a valley (trial), I must not be tithing, studying the Word enough, or praying enough. Or perhaps I'm entertaining some secret sin. The truth is we all go through valleys. It's part of God's process to bring us from glory to glory. The Bible says in 1 Peter 4:12, *"Beloved, think it not strange concerning the fiery trial which is to try you, as though some strange thing happened unto you."* II Timothy 3:12 states *"Yea, and all that will live godly in Christ Jesus **shall** suffer persecution."* Trials will come. Its part of God's pruning process. The key is to develop the proper attitude while walking **through** the valley. If we maintain our trust in the Lord and retain our peace, we will not only come out sooner, but will also become a little more like Him, as layer after layer of flesh gets peeled off.

Notice I said walk **through** the valley. Again, we have a microwave mentality. We want everything fast and easy. Some try to climb out of the valley through their own works or reasoning. Others want to run in the opposite direction, looking for a prayer line deliverance. Still others decide to just camp out in the valley and have a pity party. But, the hungry Christian, the one who is willing to suffer in the flesh to grow spiritually, will walk through the valley knowing Jesus is right there with him. Amen! The relationship grows, the faith grows, and we find ourselves one step closer to *rest*.

God knows our hearts, and He knows better than we, what we need, when we need it, and how much we can stand. Romans 8:28 says, *"All things work together for good to them that love God, to them who are the called according to His purpose."* If we believe that, then we will continue to walk through the valleys knowing that the work God is doing in us will eventually bear good fruit. Romans 8:18 says, *"For I reckon that the sufferings of this present time are not worthy to be compared with the glory which shall be revealed in us."* 2 Corinthians 5: 17 adds to this thought, *"Therefore if any man be in Christ, he is a new creature: old things are passed away; behold all things are become new."* In other words, "As the flesh goes, the Glory grows." I'll be quick to add the Glory is not for us, it is for use by the Father through us to do His work.

Now let's get back to Israel's story. Notice they speak against God and Moses. They accuse Moses of delivering them out of Egypt in order to die in the wilderness. This is still a commonly used deception of the enemy today. What we hear whispered in our ear is, "Look at what you gave up, think of what you are missing." Folks, if you really think about it, there is nothing we left behind that is of more value than our relationship with the Lord.

In verse 6 the people receive a "revelation;" they have sinned. Before a person can be saved, they first need revealed knowledge that they are lost. Many people today feel as if they are living a life just as well as "Joe Christian" next door. However true their feelings may be, it will not stand up when they face Jesus at the judgment seat. Likewise we who are truly born again need the convicting power of the Holy Spirit to keep us in check. We need to be quick to repent. Instead we tend to wait until we've already been "bitten" by the enemy.

Notice Moses acts as intercessor here, as he did several times throughout Israel's journeys. Today, according to Hebrews 7:25, Jesus *"...ever liveth to make intercession for us."* Therefore Moses is a type of Christ in this situation, but the brass serpent on the pole, what does that represent? I asked myself that same question for years. Finally I prayed and asked God to reveal the meaning to me, [If only we would learn to do this first.] While I'm sure there are other explanations, God reminded me of two scriptures. First, Genesis 3:15 where God said the "seed" would bruise the serpents head. This is the first prophetic passage concerning satans' demise by Jesus at the cross. The second scripture is found in Revelation 1:15 which describes the feet of Jesus, in His Glorified form, as "fine brass." God was demonstrating to Israel He had power over the very thing that was nipping at their heels. If Israel would recognize the omnipotence of God, they could look and live. John 3:14 and 15 bear this out. *"And as Moses lifted up the serpent in the wilderness, even so must the Son of man be lifted up: That whosoever believeth in Him should not perish, but have everlasting life."*

At this point you may be thinking, "All that's very interesting but what does that have to do with me." If you have walked the Christian life for very long at all, you have come to realize your dependence upon God. The subtle things the enemy uses to "bite" at our heels, God has authority over. Furthermore, Jesus passed on this authority on to us.

We need to look to God as our source for everything. He said He would supply all our needs, (Phil 4:19.) That includes wisdom, discernment, material needs, as well as deliverance. The valleys reveal to us what we need deliverance from. We in turn rely upon the Holy Spirit to direct us in walking it out.

Salvation is the starting point for every believer. Yet we continue in the process of growing until Jesus comes or we go to meet Him. David's' mighty men were not mighty men before they met him. They had to go through process. They came to David in their need at Adullam. Later at Hebron, David's men united with him in covenant. They were no longer "babes." They had laid aside their own aspirations in order to make David king. From that point they were able to take the stronghold of Jebus which was considered impregnable. (1Chron. 11)

If we wish to be mighty men, or mighty women, in the army of God, then we must follow their example. We must grow up; become part of a covenant body, promote unity, and learn to put others first. We must realize that most of the strongholds in our own life, our cities, and our nation cannot be overcome alone.

David did not become king overnight. Samuel anointed him several years before he ever stepped into his appointed position. The Lord had a plan for David, but David first endured process. For example, he killed a lion and a bear before he ever faced Goliath. He learned to praise God in spite of his circumstances, and he learned to put others first.

Unless we are willing to subject ourselves to process, we will fall woefully short of God's plan for our lives. You and I are not ready to tackle the strongholds over our city if we can't control our temper when someone pulls out in front of us on the highway. We all come to the Lord in our need initially. Over a period of time we begin to grow. Often, however we find a comfort zone and our development falters. Most Christians probably don't even realize their growth has been stunted. There are many levels of Christian maturity. For the purpose of this book, and in accordance with our key passage from Numbers 21, we will discuss eight levels of maturity. There are seven steps between Oboth and Pisgah. I refer to the steps as plateaus. The ultimate is Pisgah, the manifest presence of God. It takes time and patience to reach Pisgah. Two keys to arriving there are; 1) You must know where you are, and 2) You must be willing to leave. How long the journey takes will depend on you. Let's begin at Oboth and see where you are.

# Chapter 1

# OBOTH "Mumbling of the Father's Name

# CHAPTER 1

# Oboth "Mumbling of the Fathers name"

Numbers 21
10: And the children of Israel set forward, and pitched in Oboth.
11: And they journeyed from Oboth, and pitched at Ije-abarim, in the wilderness which is before Moab, toward the sun rising.
12: From thence they removed, and pitched in the valley of Zared.
13: From thence they removed, and pitched on the other side of Arnon, which is in the wilderness that cometh out of the coasts of the Amorites: for Arnon is the border of Moab, between Moab and the Amorites.
16: And from thence they went to Be'er: that is the well whereof the LORD spake unto Moses, Gather the people together, and I will give them water.
18: The princes digged the well, the nobles of the people digged it, by the direction of the lawgiver, with their staves. And from the wilderness they went to Mattanah:
19: And from Mattanah to Nahaliel: and from Nahaliel to Bamoth:

*20: And from Bamoth in the valley, that is in the country of Moab, to the top of Pisgah, which looketh toward Jeshimon.*

## A summary of Israel's' destinations; their meaning and what they represent to us spiritually

| | | |
|---|---|---|
| Oboth | "Mumbling of the Father's name" | Where we all start; as babes in Christ |
| Ijeabarim | "Ruins of the passers" | Leaving our past behind |
| Zared | "Exuberant in growth" | Growth evident in your life |
| Arnon | "Radical stream" | Zealous in your walk |
| Be'er | "A well" | Encouraging others |
| Mattanah | "A present or offering" | Laying it all on the altar |
| Bamoth | "High Elevation" | Enjoy the splendor while avoiding the pitfalls |
| Pisgah | "A cleft" | Experience the manifest presence of God |

A casual reading of Numbers 21: 10-20 would not appear as anything to get excited about. However, if given a closer look, an interesting pattern develops. When the names of the cities Israel sojourned in are defined in Hebrew, they depict the *ideal* spiritual journey of a believer. I emphasize the word ideal because this pattern is an example of the **model** Christian life. Unfortunately many never get past Oboth. We remain selfish, complaining, mumbling, stumbling, baby Christians. God help us see our need to grow up, vessels fit for Your use.

We cannot grow up if we aren't willing to cooperate with the Holy Spirit during the trials of the valley. You can rebuke them, plead with God, and practice every form of spiritual warfare you know, but the Word says "Trials will come." They are actually for our benefit. God doesn't send them, but He does allow them to show us where we are. When we respond properly we advance. When we don't, we get to take the test again. There are no shortcuts to spiritual maturity. The sooner you face the trial with the proper attitude, the sooner you will emerge from the valleys victorious.

Peter wrote *"As newborn babes, desire the sincere milk of the Word that you may grow thereby."* (1 Pet 2:2) The Greek word for "babe" is **nepios.** It means "not speaking, unsophisticated, or simple minded." Granted in the natural we can speak and may be highly intelligent when we come to Christ, but what the Word is indicating is that we need to learn a new language, mature, and develop the mind of Christ. We've been born again. We are a *"new creature, old things are passed away, behold all things are become new."* (2 Cor 5:17] That includes our speech.

Our new language isn't necessarily foreign. It is simply faith filled words based on the Word of God. The Bible says *"Faith cometh by hearing, and hearing by the Word of God."* (Rom 10:17) So as we hear the Word our faith grows. As we exercise what we learn through faith we mature as believers. At some point every believer must take responsibility for themselves. If we continue at Oboth we remain mumbling, simple minded, carnal Christians.

Babies take several years before they learn to walk, feed themselves, clothe themselves, and express themselves coherently. It is similar in the Spirit realm; however God can expedite the process if we truly desire growth. The key is exercising our faith, or as Hebrews 5:14 puts it, *"by reason of use."* Applying the Word we hear to our lives is the key to rapid Christian growth. There are no shortcuts to spiritual maturity; we will face the valleys. But how we respond to the valleys will determine the length of the journey through each one. Overcoming the trials of the valleys is what transforms us into teleios, (mature) Christians.

Jesus warned us in Matthew 7:24-27 that our spiritual house must be built upon a firm foundation. *"Therefore whosoever heareth these sayings of mine, and doeth them, I will liken him unto a wise man, which built his house upon a rock: And everyone that heareth these sayings of mine, and doeth them not, shall be likened unto a foolish man, which built his house upon the sand: And the rain descended, and the floods came, and the winds blew, and beat upon that house; and it fell. and great was the fall of it."* Without a solid foundation we become "yo-yo" Christians. We're up when everything is going well, but when the trials come and the process (valleys) seems too hard, we're knocked down. We feel overwhelmed by the circumstances of life and fail to understand what God is doing. The elements of life leave us feeling discouraged and disillusioned.

On the other hand if we are doing what God shows us in His Word, by faith, then we will become more and more stable. God wants to help us. James 1:2-8 exhorts us to retain our joy even during times of trials. *" ² My brethren, count it all joy when ye fall into divers temptations; ³ Knowing this, that the trying of your faith worketh patience.*

*⁴ But let patience have her perfect work, that ye may be perfect and entire, wanting nothing. ⁵ If any of you lack wisdom, let him ask of God, that giveth to all men liberally, and upbraideth not; and it shall be given him. ⁶ But let him ask in faith, nothing wavering. For he that wavereth is like a wave of the sea driven with the wind and tossed. [7] For let not that man think that he shall receive any thing of the Lord. [8] A double minded man is unstable in all his ways."*

Notice verse 8, the Word says if we need wisdom concerning the trial, God will grant it if we simply ask. If we respond correctly we become more stable, if not we become unstable in all our ways. The choice is yours. Do you want to build on the Rock, (Jesus) or on the sand, (flesh)? Is your desire to be stable, firmly rooted and grounded in the Word? Or will you remain a "yo-yo" Christian, up and down whenever it rains on your parade, like a toy in the hand of satan.

**\* IF TRIALS DISCOURAGE US IT'S BECAUSE WE ARE OPERATING ON OUR FEELINGS INSTEAD OF FAITH IN THE WORD \***

In 1986 I was released from Ft. Pillow prison in west Tennessee and came to a place called Miracle Lake Christian Training Center in east Tennessee. This ministry was started by a man named Jack Bryan who had a vision to help hurting men with drug and alcohol problems, some who had done jail or prison time. Jack visits the local jail weekly, and once a month visits every prison in the state of Tennessee. That is how I first came to know Jack Bryan. I looked forward to attending his service each month and recognized the wisdom and practicality of his teaching.

The parole board had stipulated I attend just such a place since I had a background involving drug use. Miracle Lake was the logical choice since I already knew Jack and respected him as a spiritual mentor. Ordinarily the program is eight weeks long, I stayed for five months. Later, I returned as assistant director and eventually served on the Board of Directors.

What I want to share with you in this chapter is based on the fundamental teachings every student at Miracle Lake is privileged to hear. These are truths that every believer should be taught as soon as possible upon their conversion. Why? Jesus emphasized the importance of a solid foundation in Matthew 24. Our study in Hebrews chapter 6 will detail the content of that foundation. The basic format of this book is plateau, valley, valley, repeat. But please bear with me in this first chapter. I believe this teaching is paramount in your Christian walk and to your success in the valleys.

## 6 FOUNDATION BLOCKS

To fully appreciate the 6 foundation blocks in chapter 6, we must first back up to the last 3 verses of chapter 5. *"For When the time you ought to be teachers, you have need that one teach you again which be the first principles of the oracles of God; and are become such as have need of milk, and not of strong meat. For every one that uses milk is unskillful in the Word of righteousness: for he is a babe. But strong meat belongeth to them that are of full age, even those who by reason of use have their senses exercised to discern both good and evil."*

Notice the reprimand given in verse 12, *"For when the time you ought to be..."* The writer is telling the Hebrew Christians that they should be teaching others. Remember that is what Be'er represents; being an encouragement, a 'well' for others. Instead they had not matured and needed to go back to kindergarten themselves. (Oboth) Without elementary education first, high school and college would be impossible. Reading and writing are not possible without knowing you're A B C's. Algebra might as well be a foreign language if you can't add, subtract, multiply, and divide.

A baby's diet consists primarily of milk. Verse 13 defines the "Nepios" Christian as one who lacks skill in the Word. Remember, a "Nepios" Christian is one who is simple, unsophisticated, and doesn't speak coherently. I stated earlier the key to rapid Christian growth was to exercise the Word in our lives as God reveals it to us. There is an old adage which says, "Use it or lose it." Today we like to use the phrase, "Just do it." The sentiment is the same expressed by the writer here in verse 14, *"By reason of use..."* Jesus said in Matthew 13:12, referring to knowledge, *"For whosoever hath, to him shall be given, and he shall have abundance."* I trust you are getting the picture. It is not enough to just know the Word; you must put it into practice. Otherwise when the rains, the winds, and the floods come, you will be swept away.

For a moment imagine that your desire is to become an Olympic athlete. Suppose I give you a manual which explains every detail required to achieve your dream of winning a gold medal. Will that guarantee your success? Even if you memorize the manual from cover to cover, the answer is no. Without implementing what you learn into your lifestyle, you will never compete in the Olympics; much less win a gold medal. The Bible isn't any different. We must **use** what we learn, apply it to our lives, or we simply become "balloon" Christians. A "balloon" Christian is one who is all blown up, (with knowledge) until the first trial comes. Then once their heart is pricked, they go flying off in 10 directions, and settle deflated upon their foundation of sand. Paul warns us of this condition in 1Corinthians 8:1, *"Knowledge puffeth up..."* Head knowledge without application = PRIDE. James 3:13 defines the alternative, *"Who is a wise man and endued with knowledge among you? Let him show out of a good conversation* *his works with meekness of wisdom."* The word conversation in this text means "behavior." A wise man doesn't just talk the talk; he walks the walk as well.

Back to Hebrews; in chapter 6 we read, *"Therefore leaving the principles of the doctrine of Christ, let us go on to perfection; not laying again the foundation of repentance from dead works, and of faith toward God, Of the doctrines of baptisms, and of the laying on of hands, and of resurrection of the dead, and of eternal judgment."* (Hebrews 6:1-3) Notice verse 1 says, "let us go on to perfection." The Greek word for "perfection" here is "*telios*" which means, "Finished, complete, mature, being used for what it was designed for." There is a vast difference between the "nepios" and the "telios" believer. The "telios" is a mature Christian, one with a firm foundation. He or she has put to use the Word they have learned. They have traversed many valleys, know who they are in Christ, and stand on the Word instead of falling on their circumstances. The fruits of the Spirit are evident in their lives, empowering the light that's within them to shine brightly. Amen!

So what is this foundation they are standing on; "Repentance, faith, lying on of hands, resurrection of the dead and eternal judgment." Notice verse 1 exhorts us to go on, yet verse 3 says, *"And this will we do, if God permit."* This indicates there are stipulations to adhere to in order to, "go on" or mature. Keep in mind what Paul wrote in 1 Corinthians 3:11, *"For other foundation can no man lay than that is laid, which is Jesus Christ."* Our job is not to lay the foundation; we are to build on it. That's why these teachings are called "The 6 Foundation Blocks." Paul warns us, *"Let every man take heed how he buildeth thereupon."* Obviously you wouldn't try to put a roof on a house if you don't have all the walls up. Yet, most of the time, that's what we attempt to do spiritually. This chapter will give you an opportunity to survey your foundation. Even if you have been a Christian for 20 years I believe you will benefit from these teachings. Make sure your foundation is solid.

There is another interesting point I'd like to share before we get into the foundation blocks concerning their order. Repentance, faith in God, and baptism all occur at or around the point of salvation. Resurrection of the dead and eternal judgment are events which will come to pass in the future. That leaves lying on of hands. Why is that one of the foundation blocks and why is it stuck there in the middle? Answer, because that's where we are now. Let me explain.

God desires unity within the body. Jesus exemplified this point when He prayed in John 17:21 *"That they all may be one as Thou, Father, art in me and I in Thee, that they also may be one in us: that the world may believe that Thou hast sent Me."* Did you catch the last part of that verse? Unity is a vital key in reaching the world with the Gospel. The Bible is specific, *"till we all come into the unity of the **Faith**."* (Eph 4:13) I don't know if there are two people anywhere who agree doctrinally on everything. Fortunately the Bible says unity of the faith... It doesn't say unity of the doctrine. We spend too much time fighting amongst ourselves to fight the real enemy, satan.

So what does unity have to do with "lying on of hands?" Everything! When we ordain ministers, send out missionaries, or pray for the sick, most often we lay hands on them. If God has called someone to the mission field, they don't need our approval, they need our support. We are simply agreeing with God's calling for their lives. Likewise when someone is sick they could pray for themselves; they don't need us, or do they? According to James 5:14 and 15, we should call for the elders to pray for the sick, why? Because God wants us to realize we all need each other. We need one another's gifts, encouragement, and support. The world says, "There is strength in numbers." Spiritually, we call this the "cooperate anointing." Lying on of hands is a foundation block because God's desire is to see a unified body.

You may notice the concept of unity interwoven throughout this book. I don't wish to be redundant; but unity is such a vital factor for the success of the end time church. Lying on of hands is where we are positionally and we are the end time church. So let's begin getting our foundation laid. Oboth is where we all begin, but there is so much more of God to experience. Let's get started.

## REPENTANCE FROM DEAD WORKS

The Greek word for repent is "metanois." Meta means, "To change" as in metamorphosis. (Change form) Nois means, "Mind." Together we have, "change of mind." I think of it this way, we've done everything our way, failed miserably, and decide to go another direction. We change our mind and decide to do it God's way. Doing it God's way, "Faith towards God," is our next foundation block. Without combining both steps we cannot effectively change. You can take a pig out of its pen, clean it up, and dress it up real nice; but when you let it go it will head straight back to the mire. His nature hasn't changed. We all start the salvation process in a state of repentance, but we can't stop there. To avoid returning to our "mire" we must truly repent, have faith in God, and believe what the Word says about us.

2Corinthians 7:10 says, *"Godly sorrow worketh repentance unto salvation."* It is possible for people to be sorry for their lifestyle, have an emotional experience, come to the altar, and leave as lost as when they came. *"Godly sorrow"* is not being sorry you got caught, or sorry you hurt someone; *"Godly sorrow"* is being grieved about being separated from the Creator. Sin separates us from God, creating a gap that only Jesus can bridge. Repentance opens the gate at the bridge, but you still must have the faith to cross over it; again, faith in God is the second foundational block.

Salvation occurs when you ask Jesus Christ into your heart. *"Therefore if any man be in Christ, he is a new creature: old things are passed away; behold all things are become new."* (2 Cor 5:17) By placing our faith in God, we receive a new nature. When we accepted Jesus Christ as our personal Savior, He bridged the gap between us and God and filled us with His Spirit. The Spirit enables us to change our nature as we renew our minds through the Word of God. Without the Spirit we become like the pig who returns to the mire.

Repentance isn't just for those seeking salvation, however. Once you receive Jesus as Lord the process continues. As you learn more about God and His goodness you realize how far you fall short. *"The goodness of God leadeth thee to repentance."* (Rom 2:4) Through the study of God's Word, teaching tapes, preaching, and other venues, we will discover issues we need to repent of; more often than not, daily. Thank God *"His mercies are new every morning."* (Lam 3:23) We are a new creation in our spirit, but our flesh is still alive and capable of rearing its ugly head. When that happens the Holy Spirit brings conviction, and we repent. We change our mind, we were wrong, and we know it. However, it seems like no time and we've fallen into the same old trap. Don't get discouraged, you may tire of your flesh, *"But His mercy endureth forever."* (Ps 136, *every verse*) Paul said, concerning his flesh, in 1Cor 15:31, *"I die daily."* We must die to our flesh daily as well, it's a slow process, but one that Paul *"counted as dung, that he might win Christ."* (Phil 3:8)

Repentance is essential in every believer's life. Romans 6:23 says *"the wages of sin is death."* While there are sins that could cause literal death, for the most part we suffer spiritual death, which is separation from God. *"But your iniquities have made a separation between you and your God, and your sins have hidden His face from you, so that He will not hear."* (Is 59:2 amplified) To ensure a good relationship with our creator, we must repent whenever we are convicted of sin. Thank the Father for His Son, Jesus Christ, who *"ever liveth to make intercession for us."* (Heb 7:25) When we repent our fellowship with God is restored. *"Our sins are cast into the depths of the sea,"* and *"as far as the east is from the west so far has He removed our transgressions from us."* (Mic7:19 and Ps 103:12)

Just how important is repentance? There are too many scripture references to discuss them all but how about 2Chronicles 7:14; *"If My people, which are called by My name, will humble themselves, and pray, and seek My face, and **turn** from their wicked ways: then will I hear from heaven, and forgive their sin, and will heal their land."* To turn is to repent, and when you turn from something you must turn to something. God is saying, "turn to Me," God is saying, "repent!" When John the Baptist came crying in the wilderness his message was, *"Repent, for the kingdom of heaven is at hand."* Jesus followed that with His first message, *"Repent, for the kingdom of heaven is at hand."* Then He sent out the twelve disciples with their first message, *"Repent for the kingdom of heaven is at hand."* It seems that God thinks repentance is pretty important, shouldn't we?

1John 1:9 is an excellent place to start when you are ready to repent, *"If we confess our sins, He is faithful and just to forgive us our sins, and to cleanse us from all unrighteousness."* Jesus is concerned about our spiritual growth. Hebrews 12:2

tells us, *"Jesus is the Author and Finisher of our faith."* What He starts He will finish, that's His promise. Amen! The Bible says Jesus, *"learned obedience by the things which He suffered."* (Heb 5:8) Should we expect any different? The valleys show us our weaknesses; our responsibility is to repent in order to grow. The good news is, if we do our part, God will certainly do His. He will give us **grace** to overcome. Grace is defined as, "the Divine influence upon the heart, and its reflection in the life." (Strong's concordance) God's grace is stronger than any sin. If we choose to repent He will give us the grace to overcome.

## FAITH TOWARDS GOD

What is faith? Webster's defines faith as: 1) Confidence or trust in a person or thing. 2) Belief that is not based on proof. 3) Belief in God or in the doctrines or teachings of religion. Personally, I like the way my friend and mentor, Jack Bryan, explains it; "Faith is eating the apple while it is still in the blossom." The Bible itself defines faith in Hebrews 11:1 like this, *"Faith is the substance of things hoped for, the evidence of things not seen."* Hebrews 11:6 goes on to say, *"But without faith it is impossible to please Him: for he that cometh to God must first believe that He is, and that He is a rewarder of them that diligently seek Him."* The truth is we all have faith; unfortunately it is usually in the wrong object. We tend to trust in our bank accounts, our jobs, relationships, etc., etc. Perhaps you aren't in a relationship, you're presently unemployed, and have no bank account; guess what, you still have faith. Do you test all your food and water for poison before consumption? Not likely, you eat and drink by faith.

In the natural we can plan, follow programs, honor traditions, and pursue our dreams. These things aren't necessarily bad; they simply are no substitute for walking in the Spirit by faith. Methods and habits do not please God because we become dependent upon them instead of Him. It pleases God when we rely on Him, which is what faith is all about.

Hebrews Chapter 11 has been dubbed, "The hall of faith," and rightfully so. Men and women of God exercised extraordinary faith in diverse ways at various times throughout history. More oft than not faith cost them their lives, yet here in America we won't even pray when we eat out because someone might see us. We rationalize that we don't want to offend anyone. America, "The Christian nation," has voted God out of the school house as well as the court house in the name of tolerance. In the guise of free religion we opted to grant witchcraft tax exempt status. The ugliest atrocity of all, however, is the taking of innocent lives and calling it pro-choice. When will we realize the farther we remove ourselves from the original intent of the Constitution, the farther we remove ourselves from God. Consequently our nation is declining in every aspect.

Over 80% of Americans claim to be Christians. Apparently we're asleep church, or ignorant; Worse yet, apathetic. Faith pleases God. We need to make a choice, continue pleasing man, or please God. The time of compromise is over. Acts 17:30 says, *"And the time of this ignorance God winked at; but now commandeth all men everywhere to repent."* There are several scriptures that teach us to obey God rather than man. To walk in faith is to please God, not man, and repent of our indifference. *"It is high time to awake out of sleep."* (Rom 13:11) The church has been a slumbering giant long enough. God wants to use us mightily in these last days, but we must be willing, and we must demonstrate faith.

So how do we build our faith? Romans 10:17 tells us, *"Faith cometh by hearing and hearing by the word of God."*

*Oboth "mumbling Of The Fathers Name"*

The Greek word for hearing implies, 'to hear and understand'. You can know the Word of God intellectually by hearing it audibly but what you need is to understand it through the inspiration of the Holy Spirit. Listen to these next two scriptures and I think you'll appreciate what I'm trying to convey. (2 Tim 3:16, 17) *"All scripture is given by inspiration of God, and is profitable for doctrine, for reproof, for correction, for instruction in righteousness."* *"But the natural man recieveth not the things of the Spirit of God: for they are foolishness unto him: neither can he know them, for they are spiritually discerned."* The Bible was written through the Spirit and must be understood through the Spirit. When the Spirit reveals truth to you and inspires you to act upon that truth, your faith grows.

While every man is dealt a measure of faith, most ignore it to entertain their flesh. Those who choose to exercise that faith are the few to whom I dedicate this book. James wrote *"Faith without works is dead,"* and went on to say two verses later *"The devils believe and tremble."* (2:17, 19) It is not enough to believe there is a God and give Him mental assent. We must develop a personal relationship with the Father, through Jesus, with the help of the Holy Spirit. Doing so motivates us, by love for God, to demonstrate our faith by our obedience.

When asked which of the commandments was greatest, Jesus replied, *"Thou shalt love the Lord thy God with all thy heart, and with all thy soul, and with all thy mind."* (Matt 22:37) Jesus also said, *"If you love me keep my commandments."* (Jn 14:15) Faith is our willingness to do what's right regardless of the circumstances, no matter how we feel, or what it's going to cost us. Galatians 5:6 says, *"Faith worketh by love."* As your relationship with your Creator grows so will your love for Him. That love will in turn propel you by faith to taste the apple while it's still in the blossom.

## Doctrine of Baptisms

There are several aspects of baptism, hence the plurality. As we are discussing foundational principles, we will address just two; Water baptism, and the baptism of the Holy Spirit. If the latter phrase frightens you, please keep an open ear. After all Romans 8:9 says, *"If any man have not the Spirit of Christ, he is none of his."* Let's begin with water baptism.

God has given us two ordinances we are to maintain, communion and water baptism. More than likely you have heard teaching on both. Yet, in my humble opinion, we take them far too lightly. Paul wrote in 1Corinthians 11:30, *"For this cause many are weak and sickly among you, and many sleep."* The word sleep in this verse is a nice way to say dead. Annanias and Saphira literally died for treating the things of God as common when they lied to the Holy Ghost. Water baptism must be taken seriously and appreciated for what it does as well as what it represents.

In some countries baptism is a sacred privilege for the believer. Candidates esteem it as the honor it is to follow the Lord in baptism. Sadly most Americans just see it as another thing on a long list of do's and don'ts. This is primarily due to a lack of proper teaching. I will not attempt to do an exhaustive teaching here, our objective is foundational; but I will probably say some things you've never considered.

Miracle Lake sponsors two full time chaplains in the Tennessee prison system; one in middle Tennessee, the other in east Tennessee. Both have reported baptizing new converts while the men were in shackles. This isn't the norm; these men were under high security. Nevertheless these inmates demonstrated that their desire to serve the Lord exceeded the misery factor involved.

Phillip was led by the Spirit to evangelize and baptize an Ethiopian eunuch in Acts 8:26. As the two conversed they came upon water. The eunuch said in verse 36, *"See, here is water; what doth hinder me to be baptized?"* You can almost feel his excitement and eagerness to obey the Lord. We should be just as exuberant. Why? First it is a command according to Matthew 28:19, *"Go ye therefore, and teach all nations, baptizing them in the name of the Father, and of the Son, and of the Holy Ghost."* Jesus said if we love Him we would keep His commandments. (Jn 14:21) Next water baptism identifies us with the death, burial, and resurrection of our Lord and Savior Jesus Christ. The third point is the one I wish to emphasize; water baptism demonstrates our power over the enemy.

1Corinthians 10:1 and 2 will serve as my text for this point, *"Moreover, brethren, I would not that you should be ignorant, how that all our fathers were under the cloud, and all passed through the sea; and were all baptized unto Moses in the cloud and in the sea."* When Israel crossed through the red sea in Exodus chapter 14 they had departed from Egypt, a shadow or type of the world. The enemy pursued them and was destroyed by the waters that had been cut off for Israel's' sake. This is symbolic of our conversion as well; we are born again, and shortly thereafter baptized.

The part about the enemy no longer having dominion over us is usually where we drop the ball. We do not have to yield to sin anymore. The enemy is cut off from our life in the sense that we are no longer a slave to sin. Romans 6:16 says it like this, *"Know ye not, that to whom ye yield yourselves servants to obey, his servants ye are to whom ye obey; whether of sin unto death, or of obedience unto righteousness."* Backing up to verse 4 of the same chapter we are exhorted to walk according to the resurrected man, the new man. *"Therefore we are buried with Him by baptism into death: that like as Christ was raised up from the dead by the glory of the Father, even so we also should walk in newness of life."* Verse 6 continues the analogy by saying, *"Knowing this, that our old man is crucified with Him, that the body of sin might be destroyed, that henceforth we should not serve sin."* Finally notice verse 7, *"For he that is dead is freed from sin."* Folks a dead man can't sin. Baptism is a picture of the old man dying, however we would be wise to follow Paul's example when he said, *"I must die daily."* (1 Cor 15:31) Also remember the enemy that held Israel captive was destroyed, yet they faced many new enemies on the other side. Baptism doesn't exempt you from facing trials; it demonstrates that you have power in them.

## BAPTISM of the HOLY SPIRIT

The phrase "baptism of the Holy Spirit" is one of the most controversial subjects in the body of Christ today. I don't propose to clear up all the controversy in a few pages here; but I will simply submit what the Bible says on the subject. You may then prayerfully meditate on the scriptures and reach your own conclusions. There is one aspect concerning the Holy Spirit that is not negotiable or optional; you are lost without Him. Romans 8:9 says *"But you are not in the flesh but in the Spirit if the Spirit of God dwell in you. Now if any man have not the Spirit of Christ, he is none of His."*

At the moment you ask Jesus Christ to be your Lord and Savior the Holy Spirit comes into your heart. In that instance you are "in the Spirit." You are saved; much like Noah was saved from the flood when he entered the ark. The Bible says God sealed the door; only those inside the ark lived.

*Oboth "mumbling Of The Fathers Name"*

Ephesians 1:13 and 14 tells us we are sealed by the Holy Spirit and He is the *earnest*, (guarantee) of our inheritance. Without the Holy Spirit we remain in the flesh; we remain lost. But if the Spirit is in you, you are His, you are saved.

Also keep in mind the meaning of the word Christ; it is not the last name of Jesus. The Greek defines Christ as, "The Anointed one." To be anointed means, "To be endowed with the Spirit through contact to an office or to a particular service." (Strong's} Every child of God has an anointing, an area in their lives the Holy Spirit empowers. Usually we call these our Spiritual gifts. A thorough reading of 1 Corinthians, chapters 12-14, will explain the various gifts and their purpose. What you will discover upon reading Paul's enlightening account of the gifts is that they are not for your entertainment, but rather to edify the body of Christ. Spiritual gifts, offices, anointing, anything God blesses you with is by His grace and for His purpose. God's desire is the furtherance of His kingdom through the Gospel. He has chosen us, through our gifts, to spread the Gospel.

In Luke 4:18, and 19, Jesus stood in the synagogue and read from Isaiah 61, *"The Spirit of the Lord is upon Me because He hath anointed Me to preach the Gospel to the poor, He hath sent Me to heal the brokenhearted. To preach deliverance to the captives, and recovering of sight to the blind, to set at liberty them that that are bruised."* Notice in this passage Isaiah wrote that the Spirit was **upon** Him. Throughout the Old Testament the Patriarchs, prophets, kings, etc., all had the Spirit upon them. It was only certain people for a specific task. God has given us a much better covenant. We have the Spirit within us; the same Spirit that raised Jesus from the dead. That is powerful!

In Jeremiah 31:31–34 God promised us this new covenant. He said *"I will put my law in their inward parts, and write it in their hearts."* When Jesus "yielded up the Ghost," according to Mathew 27:50, 51, *"the veil of the Temple was rent in twain from the top to the bottom."* This gives everyone who becomes a true believer access into the Holy of Holies where God's Spirit resides. And, where God's presence is, there is; liberty, peace, joy, protection, and so much more. Hebrews chapter four refers to this state as entering into His rest. This place with God cannot be obtained in the flesh, but only through the leadership of the Holy Spirit.

## Better Covenant

In the old covenant only the high priest, once a year, entered into the Holy of Holies. This was done to atone the sins of the people for one year by sprinkling blood upon the Mercy Seat. There was a very concise method prescribed by God for this, and if it wasn't followed the priest died. One such demand was that the priest first reach through the veil with a censor and provide a smoke screen between himself and a Holy God. This is symbolic of the blood of Jesus when God looks at us today. Without the blood of Jesus acting as our filter, we could not approach the Mercy Seat of God. But because Jesus is our High Priest the Bible says, *"let us therefore come boldly unto the Throne of Grace, that we may obtain mercy, and find grace to help in time of need."* (Heb 4:16)

Hebrews 10:9 says, *"He taketh away the first to establish the second,"* referring to the Old Testament, (covenant) and our covenant, (New Testament). Verse 15 goes on to say that *"the Holy Ghost is a witness to us,"* fulfilling the prophecy of Jeremiah 31 and restated in Hebrews 10:16, *"I will put My laws into their hearts, and in their minds will I write them."* The Holy Spirit has several functions in the life of the believer, one of which is to help us know the Father and His ways. In fact, this is why Jesus referred to Him as, "The Helper." None of us could walk victoriously without the aid of the Holy Spirit.

### Duties of the Holy Spirit

Jesus spoke of the Holy Spirit in John 14:16 as "The Comforter." The Greek word used is **parakletos**, which means, "advocate or helper." Also significant in this passage is the word *another*. The word **allos** translated as another literally means, "Another of the same kind." In other words, Jesus was saying when He went away; the Father would send another one just like Himself to help us.

In John 16:7 Jesus said, *"It is expedient for you that I go away: for if I go not away, the Comforter will not come unto you."* Why is it so important that we need the Holy Spirit as opposed to Jesus here on Earth? For one reason, let's turn to John 14:17, *"Even the Spirit of Truth; who the world can not receive, because it seeth Him not, neither knoweth Him; but ye know Him, for He dwelleth with you and shall be in you."* You see, Jesus as God in the flesh could only be one place at a time, but as God in the Spirit He can be omnipresent. That is why it was expedient that Jesus depart and send us the Holy Spirit. Now we can each enjoy His presence, regardless of the time or geological location.

Besides helping us in various ways, let's look at some other duties of the Holy Spirit. Let's begin in verse 26 of John 14, *"But the Comforter which is the Holy Ghost, whom the Father will send in My name, He shall teach you all things and bring all things to your remembrance, whatsoever I have said to you."* Notice He, the Holy Spirit, will teach you all things. Man can show you scripture and relate them one to another, but only the Holy Spirit can help you understand the scripture so that it can effectually work in you and for you.

Jesus promised His disciples that the Holy Spirit would also bring to their minds His words when they needed them. The same is true for us today. When we need help in any way, we can rely on the Word of God. That is why it is so important to memorize scripture. We can't obey scripture, claim promises, and look for guidance from the Word if we aren't familiar with it. On the other hand you could memorize the entire Bible and without the help of the Holy Spirit you will still miss the mark. We need the Holy Spirit to teach us, remind us at the opportune time to apply what we've learned, and discernment on how to do so.

John chapter 16 verses 8-14 describe other functions of the Holy Spirit:

> *(1) <u>Reprove the world of sin:</u> It is the Holy Spirit that brings conviction. Without conviction we would not realize when we were in sin. However, we must be careful not to confuse conviction with condemnation. The Holy Spirit convicts, the devil condemns.*
>
> *(2) <u>Guidance (vs 13):</u> Notice the Holy Spirit will speak to us only what He hears, just as Jesus did. So it is important for us to know His voice and listen for His instruction. This is how you walk in the Spirit and remain in the will of the Father.*
>
> *(3) <u>To Glorify Jesus (vs. 14):</u> The Father, Son, and Holy Spirit are one God in three offices. The Holy Spirit honors the Son for His blood sacrifice at Calvary.*

*Oboth "mumbling Of The Fathers Name"*

After His death and resurrection Jesus spoke again of the Holy Spirit with these instructions, *"Wait for the promise of the Father, which ye have heard of Me. For John truly baptized with water, but ye shall be baptized with the Holy Ghost not many days hence."* (Acts 1:4, 5) Verse 8 of Acts 1 also deserves our attention, *"But ye shall receive power, after that the Holy Ghost is come upon you: and ye shall be witnesses unto Me both in Jerusalem, and in all Judaea, and in Samaria, and unto the utter most parts of the earth."*

We are empowered by the Holy Ghost to be witnesses. That includes our walk as well as our talk. As I mentioned earlier, memorizing scripture is beneficial, but it is yielding to the Holy Spirit that shows forth His power in our life. You may have heard the saying, "actions speak louder than words." While it is true, every believer should strive to act like Jesus, there is a greater endeavor, our motives. Jesus said, *"out of the abundance of the heart, the mouth speaketh."* You see, we can readily talk the talk and occasionally walk the walk, but what are our motives? If we're just out to appear super spiritual, or impress our pastor or someone else, then our works are in vain. We are building our house with wood, hay, and stubble. But when we are empowered by the Holy Spirit our intentions will be pure, we will be witnesses for His glory.

There is another aspect to the power of the Holy Spirit that I would like to mention here. We saw earlier in the book of John that the Holy Spirit will seek glory for Jesus by bringing conviction to all and guiding the believer in His ways. When a person is truly yielding his or her life to the Holy Spirit, he or she will experience victory which produces a lifestyle that isn't just for show, but truly honors God. This Holy Ghost filled believer will, without saying a word, bring conviction to those around him or her. When they speak, there will be an anointing on what they say, to the point that the hearer will be impacted. That, my friends, is where we need to be. Believers empowered by the Holy Spirit to bring glory and honor to our Lord of Lord and King of Kings.

### Holy Spirit Facts through the Book of Acts

We have discussed the need for the Holy Spirit and some of His duties. Now let's look at some scripture concerning His arrival. In Acts 2:1, we find 120 disciples gathered together in a large room as instructed by Jesus. Verses 2-4say, *"And suddenly there came a sound from Heaven as of a rushing mighty wind, and it filled all the house where they were sitting. And there appeared unto them cloven tongues as of fire, and it sat upon each of them. And they were all filled with the Holy Ghost, and began to speak with other tongues as the Spirit gave them utterance."*

There are many points we could discuss about these scriptures, but let's just note the highlights.

1. They were all gathered in obedience to the command of Jesus.
2. Assembling ourselves today is still a command, not an option.
   "They were all with one accord."
   Throughout the scriptures we find the importance of unity. These people were all hungry for the promise Jesus had spoken of.
3. The Holy Spirit came on the scene in a dramatic way. Why?
   It is human instinct to explain things away if possible. We find later in the chapter where those who heard the disciples speaking in various languages assumed they were drunk. So the wind, the fire, and

the empowerment to speak in other tongues was for a witness, both to the disciples and to others that the Holy Spirit had arrived to fulfill prophecy as Peter mentioned in verses 16 – 20.
4. Notice they were **all** filled. God is not a respecter of persons. Those who truly desire a relationship with Him can be saved and filled with the Holy Spirit.

This last point was emphasized later in the same chapter beginning in verse 33. Peter had explained to the bystanders that what they were witnessing was a fulfillment of the prophecy spoken by Joel concerning the Holy Spirit being poured out. In verse 33 he summarized by saying, *"Therefore being by the right hand of God exalted, and having received of the Father the promise of the Holy Ghost, He hath shed forth this, which ye now see and hear."* The people felt convicted by Peter's words and asked him what they needed to do. Notice his reply in verses 38 – 39, *"Repent, and be baptized every one of you in the name of Jesus Christ for the remission of sins, and ye shall receive the gift of the Holy Ghost. For the promise is unto you, and to your children, and to all that are afar off, even as many as the Lord our God shall call."*

When Peter said, *"You, your children, and to all that are afar off,"* he was referring to us, and to those after us until Jesus comes. He didn't mean those in distance lands, although they were certainly included in the word "all" and "*as many as the Lord shall call.*" "*You, your children,*" is a generation, a standard time reference biblically speaking. So, again "*all that are afar off*" means us. Notice the Holy Spirit at work;

(1) He manifested Himself as a witnessing tool
(2) He led Peter in his speech

(3) He brought conviction on those who stood by

The gift of the Holy Ghost is not limited to certain people or denominations. He is meant for all. There are many people today who associate the Holy Ghost with words like, "spooky, weird, or strange." I don't wish to offend anyone, but that is just ignorance. It is natural for people to fear what they don't understand. It is supernatural to have faith in something we can't see, and believe that, "something," (Holy Spirit) enables us to live the Christian life.

In Acts chapter 4 Peter and John are taken prisoner for a day. The next morning they are brought before the religious leaders for questioning then threatened not to speak of Jesus anymore. Their reply was, "*We ought to obey God rather than men.*" Upon release they reported to the other believers of their plight. Once again we find them in one accord and once again we see something rather unusual. They didn't pray for protection, deliverance, or anything that would make it easy; they prayed for more boldness. *"And now, Lord, behold their threatenings: and grant unto Thy servants, that with all boldness they may speak Thy Word. By stretching forth Thine hand to heal; that signs and wonders may be done by the name of Thy Holy Child Jesus."* Evidently God was pleased with their prayer because in verse 31 the Bible says, "*the place was shaken where they were assembled together; and they were all filled with the Holy Ghost, and they spake the Word of God with boldness.*"

We need that type of boldness today. We have become so Heavenly minded we are no earthly good. God saved us for a purpose other than "fire insurance." Begin to pray for Holy Ghost boldness instead of deliverance and see if God won't do some shaking. Regardless of the outcome, you will be blessed when you know that you have spoken whatever God laid on your heart, boldly, yet with love.

The Bible goes on to say in verse 33, "*And with **great** power gave the apostles witness of the resurrection of the Lord Jesus: and **great** grace was upon them all.*" God is a **great** God. Through the Holy Spirit this same power and grace is available to us today. Why then do we fall so short? I believe the biggest reasons are: 1) these people were hungry for God. 2) They were united. 3) They were not full of themselves, or their own agenda. The Holy Spirit will not force Himself onto the throne of your heart. As long as you insist upon occupying it yourself, you leave no room for Him. "What must I do," you ask? Jesus said, "Only **believe**." Faith is the foundation for receiving anything from God. If you don't believe God can save you He won't; as Jack Bryan used to say, "don't worry, He won't sneak up on you and save you." Furthermore if you cannot believe that God will empower you through the Holy Spirit, just as He did the early church, He won't. **Great** power and **great** grace starts with **great** desire. How much of God do you wish to experience? How much can you believe? Finally, are you willing to serve Him when He calls?

### Obeying the Holy Spirit

In Acts chapter 9 we find the conversion of Paul. His testimony demonstrates some important principles of God.

1) <u>God can and will use anyone who is willing.</u>
Paul was given permission by the "religious" crowd to beat, imprison, or even kill anyone professing to be a follower of Jesus. This same

man went on to write approximately a third of the New Testament.

2) <u>God is a God of order and within that order is a plan for each of our lives.</u>
When Paul met the Lord on Damascus road, he wasn't told everything he would do for the rest of his life. If he were he might have ran. He was to be beaten, stoned, shipwrecked, persecuted, and imprisoned. The Lord simply told Paul to go into the city and there he would receive further instructions. If we fail to respect God's timing and order, we will be out of order. To reach our potential God leads us through process.

3) <u>You cannot reach your full potential without the aid of other believers</u>.
God showed Paul early on that he was not the "lone ranger." Ananias was instructed to seek Paul and lay hands on him that he might recover his sight. Later Paul traveled with various companions and spent time with the Apostles.

4) <u>Sharing the Gospel will increase your faith</u>.
Paul immediately after receiving the Holy Ghost was baptized and began to preach Jesus. (verses 17, 18) Verse 22 says *"Saul increased the more in strength."*

The last item I want to touch on, concerning the Holy Spirit, from the book of Acts is found in chapter 19, verse 6. *"And when Paul laid his hands upon them, the Holy Ghost came on them; and they spake with tongues and prophesied."*

Jesus said, *"Freely you have received, freely give."* Paul had received the gift of the Holy Ghost by the lying on of hands. Now we find him passing on that gift to some disciples of John who had been baptized in water but not with the Holy Ghost.

We will study the importance of "Laying on of hands" in the next lesson along with the various reasons for doing so. At this juncture I would like to bring your attention to one fact; God designed man to depend upon one another. We are all of, *"One faith, one Lord, one baptism,"* but, *"We are all members in particular of one body."* In other words, we each have a unique purpose, but we need one another to function properly. The Bible teaches us that we are the body of Christ and He is the head. Just as our brain sends electrical impulses throughout the body with instructions, Jesus sends the Holy Spirit throughout His body with direction. We need to learn to listen to and rely on the Holy Spirit. If we don't trust our hearing, or, if our legs have fallen asleep, our body will most likely fail to respond.

## Importance of Holy Spirit Led Life

For 26 years, before I was saved, I was one miserable human being. I had excuses; no father, no affirmation, little affection, etc., etc. I felt unlovable, an outcast, and inferior. I didn't even like myself. As Solomon wrote in the book of Ecclesiastes I tried everything under the sun, "But all was vanity." There is simply no substitute for the Holy Spirit in a person's life. Romans 1: 18-20 points out that all men know the truth within so that they are without excuse.

Every person is born with a void within that can only be satisfied by the presence of a loving God in the form of the Holy Spirit. When we are saved we realize the peace that passes understanding for the first time. We realize a love we never thought possible, and joy unspeakable. After the initial "honeymoon" period, we discover that while God loves us the way we are, He doesn't want us to remain the way we are. He wants us to grow up. As John the Baptist put it, *"He must increase, I must decrease."* This is a supernatural process and it takes time. In the closing pages of this study on the Holy Spirit we will discuss the importance of His role in our personal growth and development.

In Romans 8:5-8 the Bible says, *"For they that are after the flesh do mind the things of the flesh; but they that are after the Spirit the things of the Spirit. For to be carnally minded is death; but to be Spiritually minded is life and peace. Because the carnal mind is enmity against God: for it is not subject to the law of God: neither indeed can be. So then they that are in the flesh cannot please God."*

Only through the help of the Holy Spirit can we grow. Growth, or maturity, can be measured by the amount of time we spend in the Spirit as opposed to the flesh. As the passage said, *"They that are in the flesh cannot please God."* Hebrews 11:6 says, *"Without faith it is impossible to please God."* We may conclude then that walking in the Spirit is synonymous with walking by faith. Does this mean we have to be doing something "spiritual" all the time? No, we need balance in our lives. There are times when we need rest and, or, relaxation. However when God impresses you to do something, you need to respond. God will equip you with whatever is necessary to accomplish the task He asks of you. Walking, or being led by the Spirit is simply being available whenever He calls. You could think of it as a police officer on patrol. He is just cruising around when suddenly the dispatcher calls his number. He must now respond to a particular assignment. The officer was doing his job before as defined by his superiors and the law, but when something more urgent arises, he responds accordingly.

Continuing a little further, Romans 8:26 gives us another key to walking in the Spirit. *"Likewise the Spirit also helpeth our infirmities: for we know not what we should pray for as we ought: but the Spirit Itself maketh intercession for us with groanings which cannot be uttered."* There are several aspects to this verse, but because we are examining foundational principles, I wish to note only these two points:

1) When facing a trial or simply making a decision, praying with the aid of the Spirit will help us overcome the enemy and please God.
2) Praying in the Spirit according to 1 Corinthians 14:2 causes us to, *"speak mysteries in our inner man."* Simply put the Holy Spirit helps us to know the mind of God
   So praying in the Spirit is essential to walking in the Spirit. It is akin to that police officer monitoring the proper radio frequency.

There was a man who owned several dogs. Once a week he fought the dogs and took bets on which one would win. The owner bet as well, and he never lost. Finally someone asked, "How do you always know which dog will win?" "Easy," he replied, "whichever one I feed the most." The same is true of our spiritual life. *"For he that soweth to his flesh shall of the flesh reap corruption; but he that soweth to the Spirit shall of the Spirit reap life everlasting."* (Gal 6:8) You have to choose rather to feed your flesh or your spirit on a daily basis.

Just as we need the Holy Spirit to draw us unto salvation and aid us in our walk, we also need Him to sustain us. Ephesians 1:13 and 14 explain that after we hear the gospel and put our trust in Jesus, the Holy Spirit seals us. This is our guarantee to an inheritance with Jesus. Paul reiterates in Ephesians 3:16, *"That He would grant you according to the riches of His glory, to be strengthened with might by His Spirit in the inner man."* We are given of His Spirit to bring honor and glory to the Father, that His Kingdom might be advanced. That is why Jesus said wait for the promise of the Holy Ghost and you will be empowered to be witnesses. You cannot be an effective witness for Jesus without the anointing of the Holy Spirit. It is His duty to prepare the heart, guide your words, and bring conviction to the lost.

Paul continued instructing the Ephesian church on the Holy Spirit in chapter 4 verse 30, *"And grieve not the Holy Spirit of God, whereby you are sealed unto the day of redemption."* Grieving the Holy Spirit is simply not doing what He instructs you to do. Particularly if we continue in something until it becomes part of our lifestyle. God will never use a person to his or her fullest potential while bondage remains in their life. I'm not saying you can't be used, I'm saying you can't be used to your fullest potential.

God wants to use you and me for His glory, that's why He saved us. Yet most of us resent being, "used;" After all, He might *use* us in a manner in which we have no desire, or at a time which isn't convenient. If we want to walk with the power of God then we must learn to be obedient when prompted by the Holy Spirit. Philippians 2:13 says, *"For it is God which worketh in you both to will and to do of **His** good pleasure."* Paul also wrote, *"You are bought with a price: therefore glorify God in your body, and in your spirit."* (1 Corinthians 6:20) As the song says, "Jesus paid it all," it shouldn't be too much to ask for some cooperation on our part.

## Laying On Of Hands

I made the statement in the introduction that, "Lying on of hands" is where we are today as the body of Christ. I said that lying on of hands was indicative to the need we have for unity within the body. We also established, according to the Word of God, that unity was vital to effective evangelism. Is it any wonder satan stirs up strife anywhere he can? The Bible says Jesus is returning for *"a church without spot or wrinkle, or any such thing."* (Eph 5:27) Does that mean we have to be perfect? No, thank God, otherwise He would never come. What are "spots" and what do they have to do with unity? 2 Peter 2 verse 10 and verses 12-15 describe them like this, *"But chiefly them that walk after the flesh in the lust of uncleanness, and despise government. Presumptuous are they, selfwilled, they are not afraid to speak evil of dignitaries. But these, as natural brute beasts, made to be taken and destroyed, speak evil of the things that they understand not; and shall utterly perish in their own corruption; And shall receive the reward of unrighteousness, as they that count it pleasure to riot in the day time.* **Spots** *they are and blemishes, sporting themselves with their own decievings while they feast with you; Having eyes full of adultery, and that cannot cease from sin; beguiling unstable souls: an heart they have exercised with covetous practices; cursed children: Which have forsaken the right way, and are gone astray, following the way of Balaam the son of Bosor, who loved the wages of unrighteousness."*

These scriptures depict characteristics of a carnal person but at the same time say that they are in our midst. "Spots" are those who know the truth but for worldly reasons turn their backs on God. In this instance Balaam is the culprit whose name means, "Not of this people or foreigner." That should be our first clue. Balaam basically was a prophet for hire. He was in it for the money, sound familiar?

The book of Jude expands our list of spots in verses 11 and 12, *"Woe unto them! For they have gone in the way of Cain, and ran greedily after the error of Balaam for reward, and perished in the gainsaying of Core. These are spots in your feast of charity, when they feast with you, feeding themselves without fear: clouds they are without water, carried about of winds; trees whose fruit withereth, without fruit, twice dead, plucked up by the roots."*

Remember Cain, he killed his brother Abel in a jealous rage because God refused to accept what he thought was an appropriate sacrifice. There are still "brother killers" amongst us today. Why do you suppose there are so many denominations? I don't mean to get off on a tangent, but there's a word for you; Denomination, "divide the nation." So we disagree with brother "so and so," and start our own church; while we're at it lets "kill" his ministry. "We have God figured out; one day everyone will see the soundness of our doctrine. In the mean time we will pray for mercy upon these unenlightened ones, hoping they *get it* before they slip off into hell." For the most part this is an exaggeration to illustrate a point, but sadly there are those out there with just such an attitude. No one has the whole loaf. So before condemning everyone, who doesn't believe just like you, make sure you, *"first cast out the beam out of thine own eye."*

That brings us to Core. Core headed the group that attempted to take the leadership of Israel from Moses. Bad mistake; God opened up the earth and swallowed everyone who sided with him. Core represents what I like to call "church bosses." You know, the deacon that's been there since the doors were open, or the wealthiest man in the city, or perhaps the Jones family, whose numbers represent 51% of the congregation. Folks I don't care how many degrees you have or how much money is in your bank account, when God sets a man in office, the church is his responsibility. It's not a democracy. And certainly don't compound the problem by voting him out if he doesn't bend to your every whim.

Friends, I say this with all the love I can muster, spots are dangerous. In the context in which they are described, they can be false prophets, teachers, deacons, pastors, or good old boys in the pew next to you. Anyone who usurps their influence to control leadership is a potential spot. Spots are clouds without water, a form of Godliness but no power; Words with no anointing, carnal thinkers, and fruitless.

The enemy will use anyone he can to create dysfunction within the body. When the body of Christ is not functioning properly it makes little impact on the world. It becomes church as usual, stagnant and ineffective. We busy ourselves undermining the church next door while creating more programs to entertain our members.

Have you ever had the flu? Your energy is drained, everything hurts, and you don't feel like doing anything. You are so consumed with self-preservation; you certainly aren't concerned about someone else's problems. Spots are like a virus that enters the body; they infect and affect everyone in the church.

Lying on of hands is practically the opposite of spots. It may be a literal function, or symbolic, but in either case vital to the local church as well as the body of Christ. Let's look at some examples of the laying on of hands, and I think you will begin to appreciate its importance. Acts chapter 6 describes the origin of deacons. The Greek brethren were concerned that the Jews weren't ministering to their widows needs. The apostles appointed men to oversee this matter. They chose 7 men of virtue, who were wise through the Holy Ghost and laid hands on them. We still practice this act today for ordaining deacons, missionaries, and other ministerial type offices. Verse 7 of Acts 6 says, *"And the word of God increased; and the number of the disciples multiplied in Jerusalem greatly."* Unity breeds growth.

Our next example comes from Matthew 19:13-15, where we find Jesus laying hands on children to bless them. The Patriarchs had done likewise to pass down generational blessings to their sons. Many churches continue this tradition today in the form of baby dedications, or laying hands on someone at the altar as symbolic of their support.

A good example of lying on of hands to heal is found in Luke 4:40 and 41. *"Now when the sun was setting, all they that had any sick with divers diseases brought them unto Him; and He laid hands on every one of them, and healed them. And devils also came out of many, crying out and saying, Thou art Christ the Son of God. And He rebuking them suffered them not to speak: for they knew that He was Christ."* There are many instances in scripture of lying on of hands in relation to healing. I chose this example because we find both healing, and devils fleeing from the presence of Jesus. This is significant because we see that; some, not all, disease is demonically linked. Also the laying on of hands caused demonic spirits to come out of many individuals.

Well, "That was Jesus" you say, "I can't do that." Why not? The same Spirit that lives in Jesus lives in you. Why don't we see more healing? Why don't we cast out devils? The apostles did likewise after Jesus left the earth, so apparently Jesus didn't take the power with Him. In fact He said in Mark 16:17 and 18, *"And these signs shall follow them that* **believe;** *In My name shall they cast out devils; they shall speak with new tongues; They shall take up serpents; and if they drink any deadly thing it shall not harm them; they shall* *lay hands on the sick and they shall recover."* I think the key word here is **believe.** If you can't or won't believe that God will use you this way, then He won't. Jesus said in John 14:12, *"He that believeth on Me, the works that I do shall he do also; and greater works than these shall he do; because I go unto My Father."* So I ask again, what is our excuse?

I can answer that with one statement; the body of Christ is not LOUD. My wife calls me acronym man, so I'm not referring to noise here per se.

> **L**ove *is a prerequisite for unity. The body of Christ will never get past preconceived ideas, traditions, and doctrinal differences without learning to love one another.*
> **O***rder isn't an option with God either. Look at God's idea of order by these examples; Noah's ark, the altar, Tabernacle of Moses, Ark of the Covenant, and Solomon's temple. In each instance God gave specific instructions in how to build them. In each case God's design was followed and He blessed them with His manifest presence. God also presented a blueprint for the church but we haven't followed it.*
> **U***nity is not an option. We don't have to wear the same "label," conduct our services exactly alike, or have the same mission statement. The Word says, "Unity of the faith..." Love, order, and unity are synonymous, and will be prevalent in the end time church. I say that adamantly because Jesus said He was coming back for church "without spot."*
> **D***iscipleship can truly begin when we have the rest in order. Until then we will just continue to*

> *spawn duplicates of ourselves. Jesus, indeed commanded us to, "make disciples," but He said, "Teaching them to observe <u>all</u> things whatsoever I have commanded you." The church as a whole fails to disciple properly. We tend to focus on getting people saved then leave them to fend for themselves.*

I'm not saying God isn't at work. I'm saying God wants the church to be LOUD in their communities, LOUD in America, and LOUD in the world! I've seen and heard of visitations, but what we need is habitation. For that we must build the church according to His design, not our own. I say again, "Laying on of hands" is where we are in the foundation process. Without love, order, unity, and discipleship we will never look like the church Jesus died for.

## Resurrection of the dead and eternal judgment

The final two foundation blocks will be discussed together because most scripture references include both. This portion of the foundation is commonly referred to as "eschatology." That's a fancy term for "the study of end times." How do future events fit into our foundation? Without the hope of a resurrection there is little meaning to the Christian life. The choice we made to accept Jesus Christ as our Lord and Savior determined where we would spend eternity, Heaven. At the same time God protects the rights of those who choose to reject Him with their reward, hell. Understanding there is a judgment for all gives us incentive to make wise choices and improves the quality of our lives.

Theologians have been arguing over these topics since Jesus was a little boy. There are probably more books written on the subject of eschatology and end time prophecy than any other spiritual matter. My intention is not to resolve all the controversy, but rather submit to you the foundational principles necessary to graduate from Oboth.

I can still recall the joy I received from simply reading God's Word as a new Christian. I was in prison so I had a lot of time to read. It wasn't unusual for me to spend as much as six hours a day reading the Bible. I began taking Bible correspondence courses and memorizing scripture as well. The prison was old so the conditions weren't the best, but getting to know God made it more than bearable. I was happier in prison than at any other time in my life because He was with me.

I can't tell you how long it took me to read through the Bible the first time, but I read it through 12 times during my two years of incarceration. However, after the first time through, I chose to skip the book of Revelation. It wasn't too revealing to me, I didn't understand it. In 1994 I was determined to tackle the book that had mystified me for years. For nine months I studied nothing else during my quiet time except scripture associated with eschatology. Facts were easy to come by; the chronological order was a little more difficult. With the help of the Holy Spirit I arrived at some conclusions that I believe are foundational.

Let's look at a few scriptures. From Genesis to Revelation, prophecy abounds; there are many tributaries we could navigate, but we will stay with the main stream. We are concerned with laying a foundation, not charting the seas.

Jesus said, *"Verily, verily, I say unto you, he that heareth My Word, and believeth on Him that sent Me, hath everlasting life, and shall not come into condemnation; but is passed from death unto life. Verily, verily, I say unto you, the hour is coming, and now is, when the dead shall hear the voice of the Son of God: and they that hear shall live. For as the Father hath life in Himself; so hath He given to the Son to have life in Himself; And hath given Him authority to execute judgment also, because He is the Son of man. Marvel not at this: for the hour is coming, in the which all they that are in the graves shall hear His voice, And shall come forth; they that have done good, unto the resurrection of life; and they that have done evil, unto the resurrection of damnation."* (Jn 5:24-29)

According to verse 30 of that same text, Jesus is the judge. Verse 29 informed us of the criteria, our works. Rightly dividing the Word we realize it is not our works that save us. *"Not by works of righteousness which we have done, but according to His mercy He saved us."* (Titus 3:5) Reading a little further in John, (6:28, 29), Jesus answers the question what works He was referring to, *"This is the work of God, that you believe on Him whom He hath sent."* The other key elements to the verses we read in John 5 are, there will be a resurrection and there will be a judgment.

With this in mind look at Revelation 20:11-15; *"And I saw a great white throne, and Him that sat on it, from whose face the earth and the heaven fled away; and there was found no place for them. And I saw the dead, small and great, stand before God; and the books were opened: and another book was opened, which is the book of life: and the dead were judged out of those things which were written in the books, according to their works. And the sea gave up the dead which were in it; and death and hell delivered up the dead which were in them: and they were judged every man according to their works. And death and hell were cast into the lake of fire. This is the second death. And whosoever was not found written in the book of life was cast into the lake of fire."* Herein lies the outcome of the most important decision every person must make. Do you choose to believe the Gospel or not? Making no choice is the same as choosing not to believe. Denial, claiming ignorance, whatever, there is no excuse; and it won't change the facts. Heaven and hell are real and what we choose to believe in this life will determine which place we spend eternity.

Now let's look at 1 Thessalonians 4:13, 16-18), *"But I would not have you to be ignorant, brethren, concerning them which are asleep, that ye sorrow not, even as others which have no hope. For the Lord Himself, shall descend from Heaven with a shout, with the voice of the archangel, and with the trump of God: and the dead in Christ shall rise first: Then we which are alive and remain shall be caught up together with them in the clouds, to meet the Lord in the air: and so shall we ever be with the Lord. Wherefore comfort one another with these words."* There will be a resurrection for all, except as these verses point out, those believers who are alive when Jesus returns. These shall be changed *"in a moment, in the twinkling of an eye,"* according to 1 Corinthians 15:52.

One of the most comforting promises in the Bible is found in John 14, verses 1-3, *"Let not your heart be troubled: ye believe in God, believe also in Me. In My Father's house are many mansions: if it were not so, I would have told you. I go to prepare a place for you. And if I go and prepare a place for you, I will come again, and receive you unto Myself; that where I am, there you may be also."*

As stated at the outset, the resurrection, eternal judgment, and end time prophecy are the subject of numerous books. My objective is to make you aware of these important facts:

1) Jesus will return for His bride

2) There will be a judgment / one for believers and one for non-believers
3) We will each receive an eternal body and an eternal destination
4) Jesus will be our judge
5) The manifestation of the devil's defeat at the cross will culminate by satan bowing the knee before Jesus, just prior to being cast into the lake of fire along with all those who rejected Jesus as King of Kings and Lord of Lords.

For the purpose of graduating from Oboth, this is all you need to know at this time. Remember, Oboth is only the starting point; we have a long journey ahead. Ijeabarim is our first destination, our first level of growth, but to get there we must go through the valleys. That my friend is the main focus of this book; traversing the valleys successfully in order to mature as Christians. Why is it so important for us to mature? Imagine all the people you can think of who have influenced your life in a positive way; parents, teachers, relatives, friends, peers, etc. Now imagine your life without any encouragement at all from any of these sources. Much of your character would be absent; you also wouldn't be able to pass on these traits or benefit others by your experience. Paul wrote in 2 Corinthians 1:4, *"Who comforteth us in all our tribulation, that we may be able to comfort them which are in any trouble, by the comfort wherewith we ourselves are comforted of God."* Our trials are not just for us, but for future reference in aiding others in similar circumstances. Process develops character and becomes a well of wisdom to those who learn to draw from it.

Before moving into our first valley I want to reiterate that we all go through the valleys, but at different times, degrees,

*Oboth "mumbling Of The Fathers Name"*

and pace. These factors are up to you and God, He knows what you need, how much you need, and when you need it. Nevertheless, I am convinced that you will relate to each valley in your own way, and be encouraged as you learn to overcome each one. So let's turn the page and discover how we can benefit from the first valley.

# Chapter 2

# Elah
## Stronghold of the Tongue

CHAPTER 2

# The Valley of Elah "a strong tree/ as an oak"

---

Once we leave Oboth, our starting point, we head toward Ijeabarim. To get there we must pass through two valleys, Elah and Sorek. You will always find in the spirit realm that trials come before promotion. Growth should always be your objective. This will be our pattern throughout the rest of the book; two valleys before each new destination. Of course in reality there may be two, two hundred, or two thousand trials before we advance to a new level. It all depends upon how we respond to the trials. Remember it took Israel 40 years to make an eleven day journey.

You are standing at the mouth of the first valley. Before entering let's review a bit. We have been saved. At Oboth we learned some basics to build upon our foundation, Jesus. Our destination is Pisgah where the manifest presence of God abides. To get there we must go through many valleys, (process) and there are several stops along the way.

Before taking your first step into the valley, make a quality decision to complete the journey. Jesus said, *"No man builds without first counting the cost."* (Lk 14:28) Without a commitment, the enemy will cause you to stop short of your potential and settle for, what I call, "casual Christianity." The casual Christian is content in warming the pews, he has his fire insurance; he's just waiting on Jesus. Furthermore the casual Christian will be the first to criticize anyone who steps out to do anything. And he certainly doesn't want to hear any truth, so don't confuse him with the facts. Friend, it's the truth that makes you free, and if you want it, you will find it in the valleys. The question then is what will you do with it? God allows us to go through the valleys to show us the truth about ourselves; He already knows where we are. Pass the test and get promoted, fail and face it again. Are you ready for your first step... I thought so.

> *"And Saul and the men of Israel were gathered together, and pitched by the valley of Elah, and set the battle in array against the Philistines. And the Philistines stood on a mountain on the one side, and Israel stood on a mountain on the other side: and there was a valley between them. And there went out a champion out of the camp of the Philistines, named Goliath, of Gath, whose height was six cubits and a span."*
> (1 Sam 7:24)

The very nature of this valley is revealed by the names; Elah, and Goliath. The Hebrew defines Elah as, "a strong tree/ as an oak." Goliath means, "to reveal in an abrasive manner/ or to strip naked (particularly prisoners)." Based on the context of this Biblical account, I surmise that Goliath represents "the giant of the tongue," in a valley that symbolizes a stronghold. Goliath had stripped the army of Israel with his words and rendered them helpless. Words are powerful. If we listen long enough, words create avenues in our mind the enemy can capitalize on. In fact he will build an entire subdivision on one lie. A simple definition of a stronghold is, "To believe a lie to the point where it distorts our thinking." That lie becomes a filter for every decision we make.

How often have we allowed satan to immobilize us through someone's words? We have all been ridiculed, or hurt at some point in our lives. As a child, perhaps your comment was, "sticks and stones may break my bones but words will never hurt me." If only it were so. We may try to hide it, but the truth is we all take offence at some point because of verbal attacks.

David is a good example of speaking the Word but Jesus is the Word. And just to be balanced, there are times when words aren't needed. Isaiah 53:7 speaks of Jesus prophetically, *"He was oppressed and He was afflicted, yet He opened not His mouth."* When Jesus was falsely accused He didn't fight or flee, He forbear. *"For the joy that was set before Him, (Jesus) endured the cross,"* according to Hebrews 12:2. Controlling our words is an important skill to acquire. Developing the Christian walk to this extent doesn't happen overnight. But emulating Jesus in this area is vital to the maturing process. Staying focused on the prize serves as a motivator to keep you moving through the valley.

I have been inclined to vent when things don't go my way. This wasn't always well received. Some folks tended to take the venting personally, as though I were attacking them. Eventually I discovered that self-control prior to the incident is usually easier than the apology that inevitably follows. Ephesians 4:26 says, *"Be angry and sin not."* When anger is verbalized chances are it won't fall under these parameters; *"Let no corrupt communication proceed out of your mouth, but that which is good to the use of edifying, that it may administer grace unto the hearers."* (Eph 4:29)

Abrasive speech is not only hurtful to others, it hurts you as well. You cause yourself stress, invite condemnation, and perhaps mar your testimony. I heard something once that illustrates my point, "When a wise man and a foolish man argue, it's difficult to determine who is who." To mature as Christians we cannot afford to be manipulated into verbal shouting matches with others. After all, when you lose your temper, guess who finds it? If you said the devil you are correct.

Each of us has "buttons" that trigger a response based upon the strongholds we've allowed the enemy to build in our minds. By renewing the mind through the Word of God we disable the buttons so that the enemy has nothing to push. That is why Jesus could say, *"satan has nothing in Me."* (Jn 14:30) Jesus was referring to satan's efforts in the wilderness to tempt Him. Hebrews 4:15 tells us Jesus, *"was in all points tempted like as we are, yet without sin."* Jesus was tempted just as we are, but by passing the test, satan had no button to push, and no avenue to form a stronghold.

There's an old adage which states, "You can't stop the birds from flying over your head, but you can keep them from building a nest." The enemy will come to tempt you, that's a given; but you don't have to give in. Controlling our words is an important skill to acquire. Another interesting saying that applies here is, "If you give satan an inch he will want to be a ruler." Each time we allow satan to push our button the avenue widens; On the other hand, when we resist him, the "ruler" is reduced to millimeters. This valley represents the stronghold of the tongue, perhaps the most dangerous bondage of the enemy. If you want to be free of his strongholds, begin by controlling your tongue. James taught if a person could control the tongue, he could control the whole body. (James 3:2)

David learned this principle early in life, so should we. Look how David responds in this valley against the giant that we will all face. (1Sam 17:32-37) *"And David said to Saul, Let no man's heart fail because of him; thy servant will go and fight with this Philistine. And Saul said to David, Thou art not able to go against this Philistine to fight with him: for thou art but a youth, and he a man of war from his youth. And David said unto Saul, Thy servant kept his father's sheep, and there came a lion, and a bear, and took a lamb out if the flock: And I went out after him, and smote him and delivered it out of his mouth: and when he arose against me, I caught him by the beard, and smote him and slew him. Thy servant slew both the lion and the bear: and this uncircumcised Philistine shall be as one of them, seeing he has defied the armies of the living God. David said moreover, The Lord that delivered me out of the paw of the lion, and the paw of the bear, He will deliver me out of the hand of this Philistine."* David spoke his victory. He saw this as a spiritual battle between a defiant enemy and his God. In David's mind Goliath was already a defeated foe.

David asks a pertinent question in verse 29 of this same chapter *"Is there not a cause?"* David is referring to this unruly giant who stands against the army of the living God. We have a cause as well. The Bible teaches us we are to; 1) Glorify God 2) Grow into the image of Christ and 3) Evangelize. Our church refers to this mission, which is for every believer, as the "3 E's;" 1) Exalt the Father, 2) Edify the saints, and 3) Evangelize the world. Whatever the terminology, we have a purpose, a mission, or as David called it, a cause. The enemy will deter our every move to accomplish that cause. We must learn to operate on the premise that satan is a defeated foe. If you have any doubts consider 1John 3:8, which says, *"For this purpose the Son of God was manifested, that He might destroy the works of the devil."*

The only semblance of victory the devil achieves is when we allow him to use **our** tongue. Words are powerful; According to Proverbs 18:21, *"Death and life are in the power of the tongue."* The devil has no power; we on the other hand, have been created in our Father's image, and been given authority to exercise dominion over this earth. So what the enemy does is plant thoughts in our minds tempting us to say or do something contrary to the word of God. Once a word comes out of our mouth that doesn't line up with scripture, the devil uses it against us. In essence we are the prophet of our own lives. For instance; "I'm coming down with a cold," or, "I'm so dumb," or, "I'm getting blind as a bat," etc., etc. The enemy has no power until we give it to him. It is a law as real as gravity.

## ** DO NOT ALLOW THE enemy TO HINDER THE CAUSE BY LENDING him OUR TONGUE

Our words and thoughts form strongholds. I have two movies, based on true stories, about school teachers who took dysfunctional, below average students, and within a year transformed them into confident, well behaved, honor students. Both teachers were encouraging, patient, and displayed their genuine concern for their students. When you hear, "you're no good," and "you will never amount to anything," long enough, you begin to believe it. It is not enough to avoid saying the wrong things, although for most, that would be a huge improvement; we need to begin saying the right things, what the Word says about us. We must care about ourselves enough to agree with what the Bible promises to

*The Valley Of Elah "a Strong Tree/ As An Oak"*

us, and we must surround ourselves with other positive, faith filled, people, who will be an encouragement to us.

To get a glimpse of what God thinks about our words, consider Proverbs 6:16-19; *"These six things doth the Lord hate: yea, seven are an abomination unto Him: A proud look, a lying tongue, and hands that shed innocent blood, An heart that deviseth wicked imaginations, feet that be swift in running to mischief, A false witness that speaking lies, and he that soweth discord among brethren."* Take note, three of the items mentioned in these verses as things God hates involve the tongue. If you recall what we discussed earlier about God's purpose for our lives, the three "E's," you will realize why God takes our words so seriously. If we berate ourselves we are not glorifying the Father; He created us in His image. Also it is unlikely we will edify others, or influence anyone to accept Jesus as Lord and Savior. Let's consider one more passage that pertains to God's thoughts on the importance of words; *"I, (Jesus) say unto you, that every idle word that men shall speak, they shall give account thereof in the day of judgment. For by thy words thou shalt be justified, and by thy words thou shalt be condemned."* That sounds pretty serious to me.

So how do we develop self-control in this area? The preceding verses are from Matthew 12:36 and 37. Backing up to verse 35, Jesus gives us a big hint on where to start, *"A good man out of the good treasure of the heart bringeth forth good things: and an evil man out of the evil treasure bringeth forth evil things."* We begin controlling our tongue by first controlling our thoughts. The mind is like a computer, garbage in, garbage out. Romans 12:2 assures us you can be, *"transformed by the renewing of your mind."* So if we want faith filled words coming out of our mouths we must put faith filled words into our minds, chiefly, the Word of God. We will discuss the concept of mind renewal further in the next valley.

There is so much we could learn from David's life but we will focus on the practical lessons we can draw from this account in Elah. David spoke his victory beforehand. It wasn't haphazard speech designed to impress anyone. He knew God and trusted Him to show up. David knew experientially that, *"Greater is He that is in me than he that is in the world;" "The battle belongs to the Lord;"* and, *"It is not by might nor by power, but by My Spirit saith the Lord."* Before we face our giants we need to have a relationship with God, know who we are in Christ, and be skilled with our weapon. (The Word of God)

Verse 51 says David used Goliath's own sword to kill him. What the enemy means for harm God can use for our good. God enjoys turning the enemy's schemes against him. If you have never done so, read 2 Chronicles chapter 20. In a nutshell three kings come against Jehoshaphat, the king of Judah. The odds were overwhelming, inspiring Jehoshaphat to seek the Lord. He proclaimed a fast and began to pray, reminding God of His covenant. The Lord heard and sent a prophetic word which Judah obeyed. Singers went out ahead of the army singing, *"Praise the Lord for His mercy endureth forever."* The Bible records in verse 23 that two of the opposing Kings stood against the third and then turned on one another. Basically the enemies destroyed themselves, but it was God that caused them to do it because the people obeyed His direction. When God's people lift Him up, God will show up, and God will show out. He is the same yesterday, today, and forever.

The next time you feel defeated by your circumstances try praising God anyway. The enemy will be confused and turn on himself. You won't feel like it at first but as you continue

*The Valley Of Elah "a Strong Tree/ As An Oak"*

to press forward you will get a breakthrough. The sacrifice of praise will become genuine and powerful, and then the joy will come. *"The joy of the Lord is your strength."* (Nehemiah 8:10) The enemy is always trying to steal our joy because he knows there is power there. The reason there is power is because God honors faith. When we learn to praise God in spite of our circumstances, I believe our "circumstances" will become fewer and farther between. If the devil learns that every time he stirs you up you're going to have a praise party, he will visit far less often. Don't get me wrong he will come; but as we submit to God and resist the devil, the enemy has to flee.

The circumstance that looked like a giant will fall when you apply the Word mixed with faith. David spoke to his giant and it was defeated. We also must learn to speak to our giants if we desire a strong relationship with our Heavenly Father and expect any semblance of victory. Never tell God how big the giant is, tell the giant how big your God is. Amen!

I've often said that if the Bible didn't work I'd throw it away. That is a strong statement and probably seems extreme to you; but if the Word isn't true, why bother? After 34 years I can testify to its validity. Every word is true and I am constantly learning new truths. By the way, it is important that when you receive new truths, apply them. Jesus said in John 8:31 and 32, *"If you continue in My Word, then are you My disciples indeed; And you shall know the truth and the truth shall make you free."* Jesus is speaking to believers here, encouraging them to continue in the truth as it is revealed to them. Thus *"making"* them free: notice it is a process. I want to emphasize, it's the truth you <u>know</u> that makes you free. Not the words you read. We must learn to believe and apply truth the same way we accepted Jesus, "By grace through faith."

*Nahaliel The Valley of God*

This valley also serves as an example for **not** applying the truths revealed to us. Refer back to verse 4: Notice where Goliath was from, Gath. Joshua had left Gath standing when God had said, "Destroy all the inhabitants of the land from before you." This oversight led to the mocking of Israel by a giant. To reject truths, or simply not apply them, may open the door for giants in our lives. Unconquered sin will eventually create problems in our life as well as the lives of those around us.

The death of Jesus on the cross secured more than just our salvation according to Isaiah 61:1, 2. *"The Spirit of The Lord God is upon Me; because the Lord has anointed Me to preach good tidings unto the meek; He hath sent Me to bind up the brokenhearted, to proclaim liberty to the captives, and the opening of the prison to them that are bound; To proclaim the acceptable year of the Lord, and the day of vengeance of our God; to comfort all that mourn."* Jesus took back the keys to the Kingdom and gave them to us. We have authority over the devil, he is a defeated foe. We need to act like it, think like it, and talk like it! Any ground God shows us we can walk on is ours. Keep in mind this can be literal, or as it most often is, a matter of our heart condition. This valley is about overcoming giants in our lives. When faced with your giant, don't run from it, run towards it, knowing Jesus has given you the victory.

Another factor to consider is, when God reveals truth to us, we need to respond to the entire revelation, not just a portion. For instance, why did David pick up 5 smooth stones in verse 40? He only needed one, right? When you read 2 Samuel 21:15-22, which records David's life years later, you will see his mistake.

## The Valley Of Elah "a Strong Tree/ As An Oak"

*"¹⁵Moreover the Philistines had yet war again with Israel; and David went down, and his servants with him, and fought against the Philistines: and David waxed faint.*

*¹⁶And Ishbibenob, which was of the sons of the giant, the weight of whose spear weighed three hundred shekels of brass in weight, he being girded with a new sword, thought to have slain David.*

*¹⁷But Abishai the son of Zeruiah succoured him, and smote the Philistine, and killed him. Then the men of David sware unto him, saying, Thou shalt go no more out with us to battle, that thou quench not the light of Israel.*

*¹⁸And it came to pass after this, that there was again a battle with the Philistines at Gob: then Sibbechai the Hushathite slew Saph, which was of the sons of the giant.*

*¹⁹And there was again a battle in Gob with the Philistines, where Elhanan the son of Jaareoregim, a Bethlehemite, slew the brother of Goliath the Gittite, the staff of whose spear was like a weaver's beam.*

*²⁰And there was yet a battle in Gath, where was a man of great stature, that had on every hand six fingers, and on every foot six toes, four and twenty in number; and he also was born to the giant.*

*²¹And when he defied Israel, Jonathan the son of Shimeah the brother of David slew him.*

*²²These four were born to the giant in Gath, and fell by the hand of David, and by the hand of his servants."*

There appears to be a pattern involved here. God teaches us His ways, or principles through these patterns. The principle in this case is whatever God shows you to do, do quickly lest it come back to hinder you later. God is very gracious to young believers. He will provide supernatural strength to overcome a variety of bondages early in the Christian walk.

If you sense the Spirit leading in an area of personal weakness, take advantage of His help without delay.

David failed to conquer the other four giants. These giants represented 1) "Insincerity/ hypocrisy," 2) "Lust," 3) "Pride," and 4) "Powerful grasp," (greed) Please note, the names of the first three giants can be found in Strong's concordance but #4 isn't something you will find. The Lord gave me that one, I trust you can grant me that liberty. If you recall David was plagued by each of these problems later in his life. Even though God said David was a man after His own heart, David suffered greatly in his life and caused suffering in the lives of many others.

In summary, we must conquer the stronghold of the tongue as early in our Christian walk as possible. By learning to take our thoughts captive and renewing our minds through the Word, we can praise God on the journey through the valley of Elah. Exercise your faith and your authority to speak to your circumstances, knowing that God will never, "allow you to be tempted above that which you are able."

*The Valley Of Elah "a Strong Tree/ As An Oak"*

**Valley of Sorek**
**Battle field of the mind**

## Valley of Sorek ("Vine")

In July of 1977 I was subjected to the jungles of Panama while training as an army airborne ranger. I was 18 years young and in excellent physical condition. Yet, to put it mildly, the jungle was taking its toll. The humidity was almost unbearable. It took several days to acclimate. The landscape there is so undulated any hill 30 feet or less doesn't even show up on the map as elevation. The real nemesis, however, are the vines. They are so prevalent; tackling this terrain is like trying to escape from a never ending maze of giant spider webs. The degree of difficulty is compounded by darkness. The canopy of the jungle was so dense; night vision was limited to nil, even with a full Moon.

We often refer to the world as a jungle, and it can be. That is why we as Christians need to be in excellent "spiritual condition." The devil knows his time is short, so he is applying the heat, making trials seem impossible. He entangles us in the vines and attempts to keep us in darkness.

Thanks be unto *God "Who hath delivered us from the power of darkness, and hath translated us into the Kingdom of His dear Son:"* (Jesus) (Colossians 1: 13.) We are no longer ignorant of the enemies' devices; we have the Holy Spirit within us. *"Greater is he that is within us than he that is in the world."* (1 John 4:4) We must learn to rely on our point man, the Holy Spirit to guide us through the jungles of life. The vines will still grab out at us in an effort to bind us up mentally; a condition known as a "stronghold" of the mind.

In our last valley we talked about the stronghold of the tongue. In this valley we will discuss the strongholds of the mind. Strongholds are mind sets, or patterns, we have developed during the course of our lives, through which we filter every thought or decision. Hebrews 4: 12 says *"The word of God is quick and powerful and sharper than any two edged sword, even to the dividing asunder of soul and spirit, and of the joints and marrow, and is a discerner of the thoughts and intents of the heart."* It is the word of God that acts as our machete, cutting us free from any bondage produced by the vines of the enemy.

As we continue on our journey from Oboth to Ijiabarim through the valleys let's not forget what we've learned about our foundation. Remember the "use it or lose it" principle. Once we receive what Jesus did for us at Calvary, by faith, we must then act on the Word. John 8: 31 and 32 says *"If ye continue in My Word, you are my disciples indeed. And you shall know the truth and the truth shall make you free."* As we use the Word to cut our way through the jungles of life we become free from strongholds, one vine, one thought, at a time.

Another point to ponder is, the harder you struggle the more entangled you become. Expending great amounts of energy in such a hostile environment can be very frustrating.

*The Valley Of Elah "a Strong Tree/ As An Oak"*

You must be patient in order to extricate yourself from the snares of the enemy, one thought at a time. Often help is necessary to expedite the process. Good relationships with other believers are vital to our progress toward maturity. Struggling on our own is equivalent to the works of the flesh. As long as you continue to try it your way, God will refrain from assisting you. Remember the six foundation blocks. Lying on of hands teaches us that we all need each other.

If you wish to be a successful soldier you must learn to adapt. 2 Timothy 2: 3, 4 *"Thou therefore endure hardness as a good soldier of Jesus Christ. No man that warreth entangleth himself with the affairs of this life; that he may please him who have chosen him to be a soldier."* Learn to thrive in the jungle. It is simply making a quality choice that no matter what vines the enemy throws at you, you will use your sword (Word of God) to overcome. The Bible says we are more than conquerors…; and that we overcome by the blood and the word of our testimony. I must reiterate here; Jesus won the victory at Calvary. Our responsibility lies with our testimony. Again, words are powerful!

In other words, to get through the valley of Sorek successfully we must; 1) know who we are in Christ and understand His blood has, (past tense), delivered us. 2) Secondly we must speak the Word to our circumstances so that we have a *testimony*. Griping about our circumstances to God, expecting Him to react to something he's given us the authority to do, will cause us to fail the test and leave us with the "*moanies*."

No illustration I could give would be as effective as what God's Word has recorded. So let's look at the scriptures that this valley was derived from. *"And it came to pass afterward, that he loved a woman in the valley of Sorek, whose name was Delilah. And the lords of the Philistines came up unto her, and said unto her, entice him, and see wherein his great strength lieth, and by what means we may prevail against him, that we may bind him to afflict him: and we will give thee every one of us eleven hundred pieces of silver."*

*"And it came to pass, when she pressed him daily with her words, and urged him, so that his soul was vexed unto death; that he told her all his heart and said unto her, there hath not come a razor upon mine head; for I have been a Nazarite unto God from my mother's womb: if I be shaven, then my strength will go from me, and I shall become weak, and be like any other man. And when Delilah saw that he had told her all his heart, she sent and called for the lords of the Philistines saying, come up this once, for he hath showed me all his heart. Then the lords of the Philistines came up unto her, and brought money in their hand. And she made him sleep up on her knees; and she called for a man, and she caused him to shave off the seven locks of his head; as she began to afflict him, and his strength went from him. And she said, the Philistines be upon thee, Samson. And he awoke out of his sleep, and said I will go out as at other times before, and shake myself. And he wist not that the Lord was departed from him."*

Samson was anointed of God from birth to deliver Israel from bondage (Judges 13: 5.) After killing one thousand Philistines with the jawbone of a donkey, Samson became judge of Israel, (Judges 15: 20) and an enemy of the Philistines. Judges 16: 2 exposes the plot of Samson's enemies to destroy him.

In our first key passage we find the name of the valley we are discussing. Sorek means "Vine." Next we have Delilah which means "to slacken or make feeble." The names alone tell the story. Samson, (Sunlight) becomes entangled in a vine that makes him weak and brings darkness to his soul, physically and spiritually.

God created us to be attracted to the opposite sex. The devil wants to pervert everything about God's creation. So although Samson's attraction to women was natural, his relationship with this woman was perverted. Verse 16 tells us that she pressured him daily until his mind was "vexed (discouraged, grieved, troubled, cut down). This same word was used to describe Lots condition during his stay in Sodom. 2 Peter 2: 8 says *"For that righteous man dwelling among them, in seeing and hearing, vexed his righteous soul from day to day with their unlawful deeds."*

Delilah was being used of the enemy to weaken and eventually compromise the integrity of Israel's judge, Samson. Being attracted to anything that is not God appointed will cause us to stumble. By God appointed I simply mean in His will. A Delilah doesn't have to be a woman. What presses you for your time? Attention? Money? These things can become idols and hinder our relationship with the Father, leaving us weak, spiritually blind and even in bondage.

Verse 17 reveals Samson's error. "He told her all his heart." Jesus warned us in Matthew 7: 6, *"Give not that which is Holy unto the dogs, neither cast ye your pearls before swine, lest they trample them under their feet, and turn again and rend you."* In todays "hip" terminology we might say, "Don't put your business in the street," or simply put, "you can't trust just any one to confide in." Let me quickly add I believe a Christian should maintain an open book lifestyle. Also we are to confess our faults one to another (James 5: 16). In context however, this will be with mentors, mature believers, Christian counselors, etc. Not to the world and particularly not to the enemy. Negative confessions give ground to the enemy.

One of the Bible's saddest comments is found in verse 20 *"and he knew not that the Lord was departed from him."* It has been said that 75% of the church would not recognize if the Holy Spirit departed from the earth. Folks this is a dangerous position that we find ourselves in as the body of Christ. It implies that we have learned to play church so well we can entertain ourselves in worship; be theological, while maintaining a sincere cry in prayer, and get pumped up with a sermon that seems hot off the press, (most likely the press of our own thinking.) It looks and feels like church, what's the problem? Without The Holy Spirit in the lead, we are making our own way. There is no anointing to break yokes, heal, deliver, and convict of the need for salvation. My point, be among the 25% that **does** recognize the presence of the Holy Spirit and learn to be led by Him.

You will need to develop your relationship with God through the Holy Spirit. To conquer the valleys will require the wisdom that only the Holy Spirit can communicate to you. *"If any of you lack wisdom, let him ask of God, that giveth to all men liberally, and upbraideth not; and it shall be given him."* Don't make the same mistakes as Samson. Seek the Lord's leadership at all times, but especially during trials.

**\* Don't flirt with the world on the way to the wedding \***

Verse 30 brings out another important aspect of Samson's life; he repented. In Oboth, during the six foundation blocks teaching, we discussed the importance of repentance, so I won't linger here long. Notice that through repentance and prayer Samson accomplished more through his death than he had in his life. Matthew 10: 39 says *"He that findeth his life shall lose it: and he that loseth his life for my sake shall find it."*

You do not have to literally die like Samson, but if you wish to graduate Sorek, and move from Oboth to Ijeabarim, then you will have to die to some flesh. Then, just as Samson, you will accomplish more; actually God will accomplish more through you. John the Baptist said *"He must increase, I must decrease."* It is no different for us today.

Pride, the love of money, and wrongful lusts are mankind's biggest downfall. Avoid the entanglements of Sorek. Use your "sword" to clear a path through the vines and keep walking.

# Chapter 3

# IJEABARIM
## "Ruins of the Passers"

# CHAPTER 3
# IJEABARIM "Ruins of the Passers")

The word Ijeabarim was used just twice in the Bible; both times in the book of Numbers. Both times a seemingly insignificant reference to a stopping place during Israel's early travels. This stage, stage two in our spiritual journey, is anything but insignificant. The word literally means, "Ruins of the passers."

In my mind I picture an old junk yard. Each item of refuse represents sin or bondage of the past. As we pass through the ruins, we leave behind a lifestyle of bondage. We have put off yesterday's rags and inherited His, Jesus, robe of righteousness. *"If any man be in Christ, he is a new creature: old things are passed away; behold all things are become new."* (2 Cor 8:17) We have a clean slate. *"There is therefore now no condemnation to them which are in Christ Jesus, who walk not after the flesh, but after the Spirit."* (Rom8:1) We have no guilt or shame baggage to carry. *"Brethren I count not myself to have apprehended: but this one thing I do, forgetting those things which are behind, and reaching forth unto those things which are before, I press toward the mark for the prize of the high calling of God in Christ Jesus."* (Phil 3:13, 14) We have a new future with better goals.

We have graduated from Oboth and we're pressing towards the mark, "Pisgah." Pisgah is a shadow of the Holy of Holies, a place of rest, where the Glory of God resides. As you might recall only the high priest could enter the Holy of Holies once a year to atone the sins of the people. He would tie a rope to his ankle and had bells attached to his robe so that the other priests could hear his movements. If he faltered in his duties or had sin in his life he would die. The others would then pull him out using the rope. If we desire to enter the Holy of Holies, then we must be willing to follow the leading of the Holy Spirit. We must be willing to die to some flesh. The Bible says *"For I reckon that the sufferings of this present time are not worthy to be compared with the glory which shall be revealed in us."* (Rom 8:18) Within the veil, in the presence of God, lies healing, prosperity, peace and rest. If we continue to "press towards the mark" we can enter in. We can experience the joy of being in the presence of our Creator.

The book of Hebrews tells us there remains a rest for us. It is not referring to heaven, but rather a state of mind we can attain when our faith reaches the point that we fully trust God. In other words, no matter what situation we find ourselves in we believe, *"All things work together for good to them that love God, to them who are the called according to His purpose."* (Rom 8:28) To be honest I don't believe any of us operate at that level consistently. Yet, the Bible says we can. I don't wish to discuss too much about Pisgah at this juncture, that's the seventh plateau, we're at the second. I simply want to dangle a little bait to keep you motivated because there are more valleys just ahead.

While Oboth, represents salvation, Ijeabarim is symbolic of baptism. You may recall in our teaching of the six foundation blocks we discussed baptism and its significance. Remember Israel passing through the red sea and the enemy being cut off behind them? There is a similar picture here at level two, "ruins of the passers." We leave our baggage, (old man's sins) behind. They are ruins, things that will hinder our walk.

Paul said in Hebrews 12:1 *"Wherefore seeing we also are compassed about with so great a cloud of witnesses let us to lay aside every weight, and the sin which doth so easily beset us and let us run with patience the race that is set before us."* Weights are not necessarily sins; they can be anything that restricts our maturing process. If we want to grow in Christ, we must be willing to put off and leave behind the old man. Then put on the new man. Ephesians 4:22-24 says it like this, *" That ye put off concerning the former conversation the old man, which is corrupt according to the deceitful lusts; And be renewed in the spirit of your mind; And that ye put on the new man, which after God is created in righteousness and true holiness."* Notice, <u>you</u> put off, <u>you</u> put on. Growth is our responsibility. Also note, growth comes through renewing your mind. And I might add, renewing your mind through the Word of God with the aid of the Holy Spirit.

One of satan's most effective schemes against the believer is to get you thinking, "I've done my part, I'll just go to church and bide my time." And "I've been saved and baptized, my problems are over, right? Wrong! The devil will have effectively rendered you as an unproductive member of the body. I said it earlier but it bears repeating; satan's number one goal is to destroy you before you get saved. Number two, he wants to keep you from growing into a mature Christian and discipling others.

As you exit Ijeabarim and enter the next valley check your attitude about the ruins you are passing by. Is it an attitude of sorrow and regret, or is it one of relief and joy? The enemy would like you to think you're leaving something of value behind. Or perhaps he will bombard your senses with memories of the "good times." I know personally that I have recalled some things of the past that appeal to my emotions. That's why we can't be led by our emotions. We must be led by the Spirit and we won't fulfill the lust of the flesh. Besides, I can always counter the enemy when he comes at me in this manner with memories of similar circumstances without such a desirable outcome. He doesn't bring those up unless he's already trapped you, and then it is just to pile on the guilt and condemnation.

Understand the necessity of laying it all down. Our God is a merciful God. He convicts, but never condemns as long as we are one of His children. That is why we call Him Lord. The Greek defines Lord as, "Supreme, controller, and master." In order to make more room for Him, we must empty ourselves of all the ruins. You have arrived at Ijeabarim. Herein lies a key steppingstone. Before you depart be sure you have slain your "giants," and cut all your "vines." You will need to be free and courageous because you are about to enter "The valley of the shadow of death."

*Ijeabarim "ruins Of The Passers")*

**Valley of the Shadow of Death**

**Dying to the Flesh**

### The Valley of the Shadow of Death (#3)

How often have you heard these words quoted during ominous circumstances, "Yea, though I walk through the valley of the shadow of death...?" While the words of this Psalm may be used contextually in this manner, I would like to share a couple of other aspects of the verse with you.

Psalm 23 is one of the most quoted passages of the entire Bible. You hear it recited frequently during perilous times in the movies, and yes, at gravesites. Still the majority of those who quote it are doing so without regard to the context in which it was actually written. David is bragging on Jehovah Rohi, the "Good Shepherd." David begins Psalm 23 by declaring the provision, rest, and peace that God supplies. He is boasting of God's ability as the Good Shepherd. When the transition is made to the valley, God continues to display His loving kindness as protector and comforter. *"Yea, though I walk through the valley of the shadow of death, I will fear no evil: for thou art with me; thy rod and thy staff they comfort me."* In essence David is presenting the pattern that I am using for this book; rest, valley, then rest. But please take note that even in the valley, God is there. Hebrews 13:5 confirms this characteristic of God, *"I will never leave thee or forsake thee…"*

David ends the Psalm by saying he is blessed, anointed, and has a sure dwelling place. We have inherited those same promises; *"Jesus Christ the same yesterday, and to day, and for ever."* (Heb13:8) What the Lord did for David He will do for you. You are blessed, anointed, and have Heaven as your home. *"But my God shall supply <u>all</u> your need according to his riches in glory by Christ Jesus."* (Phil 4:19) I underlined the word *all* to emphasize God's desire to care for your every need regardless of your current spiritual condition. We're discussing a valley here, but it is important to realize He never leaves us nor forsakes us. (Heb 13:5)

Whether you're on the mountain top or in the valley God is with you. He watched over David and He will watch over you. You may feel like God doesn't care at times, and there will be seasons where He seems distant; leaving you lonely in the valley. Yet, *"To everything there is a season, and a time to every purpose under the heaven."* (Ecclesiastes 3:1) It's in the valleys that we grow to trust Him more. So even if you *feel* abandoned, know that God has a reason for the season you are in. Don't give in to the devil because of your feelings. Feelings are temporal; faith endures.

Some valleys are tougher than others, but there is help available and a resting place just ahead. *"Fear thou not; for I am with thee: be not dismayed; for I am thy God: I will strengthen thee; yea, I will help thee; yea, I will uphold*

*Ijeabarim "ruins Of The Passers")*

*thee with the right hand of my righteousness."* (Isaiah 41:10) When David said, *"Yea, though I walk through the valley of the shadow of death, I will fear no evil: for thou art with me; thy rod and thy staff they comfort me"* he was speaking from experience. David understood the common denominator in these two verses; *fear not, God is with you.* Fear is the opposite of faith and the enemy's number one tool to defeat you in the valley.

Do not give in to fear in this valley; death is only a shadow. A shadow is simply a type, picture, or image of the real. David isn't necessarily referring to literal death. There are three applications possible here:

| | |
|---|---|
| 1) Spiritually dead | Those without Christ as their personal Savior |
| 2) Physical death of the believer | We have eternal life; physical death is a shadow |
| 3) Spiritual death of the believer's flesh | Renewing of the mind |

## Spiritually dead

When Adam sinned in the garden, he relinquished his God given dominion of the earth. He then passed on the sin nature through his seed. This act of rebellion initiated what is now referred to as the "Adamic nature." Romans 5:12 states it like this, *"Wherefore by one man sin entered into the world, and death by sin; and so death passed upon all men, for that all have sinned."* It's clear David understood this principle when he wrote these words in Psalm 51:5, *"Behold I was shapen in iniquity; and in sin did my mother conceive me."*

Before we are saved, we are spiritually dead; and cannot come to God through our own works or efforts. Romans 3:23

says, *"For all have sinned, and come short of the glory of God."* Romans 6:23 goes on to say, *" For the wages of sin is death; but the gift of God is eternal life through Jesus Christ our Lord."* We need a Savior, we need Jesus.

Not only are we all born sinners and spiritually dead, it is obvious we don't grow out of this position on our own. When one man asked Jesus to wait on him while he went to bury his father, Jesus said, *"Let the dead bury the dead...Follow Me."* (Matt 8:22) Jesus wasn't referring to ghosts; He simply meant the people burying the man's father were spiritually dead. Again, because Adam sinned, the people burying the dead man were as dead as he was. Fortunately, there is an answer to this dilemma, Jesus. *"For as by one man's disobedience many were made sinners, so by the obedience of one shall many be made righteous".* (Rom 5:19)

As we see in the second half of this scripture no one except Jesus has ever lived a perfect life. Because Jesus obeyed the law perfectly, we have the opportunity to become righteous in God the Father's eyes. Accepting Jesus as our Lord and Savior positions us in right standing with the Creator of the universe.

The other half of the equation is that Jesus didn't inherit the Adamic nature. This is possible because Jesus had no earthly father. The seed lies within the man; Adam passed it down from generation to generation. Jesus did not inherit the sin nature like man did. He still had the opportunity to sin through the temptations of satan but Jesus refused to do so. *"For we have not an high priest which cannot be touched with the feeling of our infirmities; but was in all points tempted like as we are, yet without sin."* (Heb 4:15) Jesus faced the lust of the flesh, the lust of the eye, and the pride of life, just as we do, but he passed the test with a perfect score. Jesus was

*Ijeabarim "ruins Of The Passers")*

able to do this with the aid of the Holy Spirit. We to can benefit greatly by relying on the Holy Spirit in our Christian walk.

John chapter 14 describes the ministry of the Holy Spirit as a comforter, teacher, and guide. A spiritually dead person will go through the valleys just like a Christian does, only without the aid of the Holy Spirit or the Word of God. 1 Corinthians 2:14 says, " *But the natural man receiveth not the things of the Spirit of God: for they are foolishness unto him: neither can he know them, because they are spiritually discerned.*" I've always said Christians are the only people living in reality. Spiritually dead people merely exist. A lost person is just that, lost. They may appear to have it all together but they are ignorant of the spiritual reality of judgement and hell.

Lost people have the attitude of a certain rich man in Luke chapter 12 who said, " *Soul, thou hast much goods laid up for many years; take thine ease, eat, drink, and be merry.*" But God replied to the rich man in verse 20, *"Thou fool, this night thy soul shall be required of thee."* The old saying, "you can't take it with you" is applicable here. Heaven trumps anything the earth has to offer. In His sermon on the mount, in Matthew 6, Jesus said it like this, *19 Lay not up for yourselves treasures upon earth, where moth and rust doth corrupt, and where thieves break through and steal:20 But lay up for yourselves treasures in heaven, where neither moth nor rust doth corrupt, and where thieves do not break through nor steal:21 For where your treasure is, there will your heart be also.*

The answer lies in the second half of a verse we mentioned earlier, Romans 6:23, " *but the gift of God is eternal life through Jesus Christ our Lord.*" Eternal security is far superior to anything we can acquire in this life. Furthermore, God is not against you having stuff, He just doesn't want the stuff to have you. He promises us in Matthew 6:33, *"But seek ye first the kingdom of God, and his righteousness; and all these things shall be added unto you."*

Jesus is the only way to righteousness; He said, "*I am the way, the truth, and the life: no man cometh unto the Father, but by me.*" (Jn14:6) Isaiah 43:11 emphasizes this point, "*I, even I, am the LORD; and beside me there is no saviour.*" I've heard many variations of the expression, "I wouldn't get caught dead…" but the worst possible scenario in life would be to get caught dead spiritually. I mean there is no do-over or second chances, no reset button.

I believe I should extend an invitation to the 'spiritually dead' at this juncture of the book. If you have read this far and still fail to see your need for salvation, I pray you do so soon. No one will ever have perfect peace nor enter the gates of Heaven without receiving Jesus Christ as their personal savior. Take the time to ask Jesus into your heart. It is the best and most important decision you will ever make. There isn't a formula, just use your own words. I was alone in my mother's house when I asked Jesus to save me on November 15, 1984, and I have never doubted my salvation.

## Physical Death

"*It is appointed unto men once to die, but after this the judgment.*" (Heb 9:27) Believers, as well as non-believers have, and will continue to die physically until Jesus returns. The decision to accept or reject Jesus Christ as personal Lord and Savior is the lone factor that determines where we will spend eternity, Heaven or hell.

For the believer death is sweet. Paul said, "*To be absent from the body is to be present with the Lord.*" (2 Cor 5:8) John was inspired to add these words in Revelation 14:13, "*And I heard a voice from heaven saying unto me, Write, Blessed*

*Ijeabarim "ruins Of The Passers")*

*are the dead which die in the Lord from henceforth: Yea, saith the Spirit, that they may rest from their labours; and their works do follow them."* The Lord is compassionate during these times as implied in Psalm 116:15, " *Precious in the sight of the LORD is the death of his saints."*

A contrast of physical death between the Christian and the lost person is best depicted by an account Jesus shares in Luke 16. Apparently there was a rich man who died about the same time as a beggar named Lazarus. The rich man went to hell, not for being rich, but for living selfishly and failing to acknowledge God. There he cried, *"Father Abraham, have mercy on me, and send Lazarus, that he may dip the tip of his finger in water, and cool my tongue; for I am tormented in this flame."* This passage is clear; hell is full of torment and flames. It shouldn't be confused with the flippant statement, "I'm on my way to hell to party with my friends." A more accurate assessment is the bumper sticker that states, "Party in hell canceled due to fire." You will also find that the rich man knew who Lazarus was and where he was.

When the wealthy man was denied his request for water, he made an interesting plea; *"I pray thee therefore, father, that thou wouldest send him to my father's house: For I have five brethren; that he may testify unto them, lest they also come into this place of torment."* (Lk 16:28) It seems the adage; "Misery loves company" didn't apply in this situation. Hell was more than he wanted for anyone he knew to bear. Indeed, I believe if we had a clear understanding of how awful hell is, we wouldn't want anyone to go there. Perhaps we would all be better witnesses.

## Death to the Flesh

This is the place within this valley that I want to emphasize. This is where we all struggle as Christians. Dying to the flesh is not a pleasant experience, but necessary if we wish to mature as believers.

A friend of mine, a contemporary Christian artist, wrote a song called, "More of You." I was having a rough time at work one day and began to listen in my mind to my friend, Todd Day, sing the words of this beautiful song. "Here I am with my arms open wide. I'm crying out for more of You." The Lord interrupted quite abruptly and said, "If you want more of me, you must have less of you." How true! It was John the Baptist who said, "He must increase, I must decrease." Dying to the flesh is about less of us and more of Him. Amen!

Romans 6:6 says, "*Knowing this, that our old man is crucified with him, that the body of sin might be destroyed, that henceforth we should not serve sin.*" Verse 16 of the same chapter goes on to say we are servants, or slaves to either death, (separation from God) or obedience, (submitting to righteousness). In other words before salvation a person is merely a puppet in satan's hands. Once we're born again we are free from him, readily able to serve God. Sin then becomes a choice. That's why Paul said in Romans 13:14, "*But put ye on the Lord Jesus Christ, and make not provision for the flesh, to fulfil the lusts thereof.*" Paul is exhorting us to avoid any situation where we might be tempted to sin. Stay away from old friends who still practice sins that were a weakness for you. Don't watch 'R' rated movies or attend gatherings where you know drug or alcohol use to be tolerated.

"*Abstain from all appearance of evil.*" (1 Thess. 5:22) Wise counsel for anyone serious about 'dying to the flesh.' 'Dying to the flesh' is a process, it won't happen overnight. Actually

*Ijeabarim "ruins Of The Passers")*

you will never completely die to your flesh in a lifetime. We will still be working on it until Jesus comes or we die literally. Don't be discouraged though, the process is slow and even painful at times, but very rewarding.

The word, "conformed" is used only twice in the entire Bible. First in Romans 8:29, where Paul says we are "to be conformed to the image of" Jesus. This word in the Greek is 'summorphos,' which means, "jointly formed or fashioned like." In the proceeding verse, Romans 8:28, we read, *"That all things work together for good to them that love God."* What Paul wants us to understand is that it's the trials, the valleys, which fashion us into the likeness of Jesus. When an artist was asked how he created his lifelike statues, he replied, "I simply chisel off everything that doesn't look like the image I see in my head." God allows the valleys in our lives to chip off everything about us that doesn't express the character of Christ.

The second time the word "conformed" is used is found in Romans 12:2. The Greek word here is "suschematizo," which means, "Fashioned after the same pattern." For better understanding of the context in which it is written, let's back up to verse 1. *"I beseech you therefore, brethren, by the mercies of God, that ye present your bodies a living sacrifice, holy, acceptable unto God, which is your reasonable service."* Now verse 2, *"And be not conformed to this world: but be ye transformed by the renewing of your mind, that ye may prove what is that good, and acceptable, and perfect, will of God."* You see, according to God's great mercy, all that He's provided through His Son Jesus Christ, we should be willing to give ourselves to Him wholly. It is only reasonable that we serve Him considering all that He has done for us. In order to do so He implores us not to fashion ourselves after the pattern of the world.

2 Corinthians 6:14 urges us, *"Be ye not unequally yoked together with unbelievers:"* and verse 17 adds, *"Wherefore come out from among them, and be ye separate, saith the Lord."* Does that mean never associate with unbelievers? Of course not; else how could we work, or more importantly, evangelize. What God desires is that we don't adopt the 'world system,' or allow secular influence to infect our character. We are to be transformed by the renewing of our mind. Reprogram your 'computer' by God's standards as outlined in His Word. When referring to the church in Ephesians 5:26, Paul wrote, *"That he might sanctify and cleanse **it** with the washing of water by the word"* "**It**," is us!

Jesus said in John 8:31, *"If ye continue in my word, then are ye my disciples indeed;* **8:32** *And ye shall know the truth, and the truth shall make you free."* The Word of God is truth. As we study it, meditate on it, and begin to apply it to our lives, our mind is transformed. It is a continual process that often seems too slow and painful. Nevertheless, the rewards far outweigh the sacrifices. 2Peter 1:2 reveals two of the benefits, *"**Grace and peace** be multiplied unto you through the knowledge of God, and of Jesus our Lord."* This verse could easily read, "The power of God displayed in your life and peace that exceeds understanding to the nth factor due to your relationship with God through His Son Jesus Christ." Abundant life comes through abundant relationship. Jesus is the Word, Jesus is the Life, and it is Jesus that can make you free! The catch is we have to want to be free; we have to want the truth.

Most of us would rather judge others than ourselves, yet 1 Corinthians 11:31 tells us, *"If we would judge ourselves, we should not be judged."* The reason we like to look at others faults instead of our own is simply that it makes us feel better about ourselves. Paul warns in 2 Corinthians 10:12, *"but they*

*Ijeabarim "ruins Of The Passers")*

*measuring themselves by themselves, and comparing themselves among themselves, are not wise."* We are all unique; we have different strengths and weaknesses. Just because you don't do what 'so and so' does doesn't mean that you are more mature than they are. Perhaps they don't struggle with some of the things that you do. I love reading church signs. I noticed one recently that said, "Don't judge me just because my sin is different than yours." Always remember Jesus is the measuring stick, not others.

## New Testament "Shadow"

As I mentioned at the outset, this book was spawned out of a Sunday school lesson. While studying for "The valley of the shadow of death" the Lord led me to Luke 1:74-80. **1:74** *"That he would grant unto us, that we being delivered out of the hand of our enemies might serve him without fear,* **1:75** *In holiness and righteousness before him, all the days of our life.* **1:76** *And thou, child, shalt be called the prophet of the Highest: for thou shalt go before the face of the Lord to prepare his ways;* **1:77** *To give knowledge of salvation unto his people by the remission of their sins,* **1:78** *Through the tender mercy of our God; whereby the dayspring from on high hath visited us,* **1:79** *To give light to them that sit in darkness and in the shadow of death, to guide our feet into the way of peace.* **1:80** *And the child grew, and waxed strong in spirit, and was in the deserts till the day of his shewing unto Israel."*

Although these verses are in reference to John the Baptist, the charge remains the same for us today. John prepared the way for the first coming of Jesus and we shall prepare the way for His second coming. What does this preparation entail and how does it apply to us?

*Nahaliel The Valley of God*

Isaiah 40:3, 4 say, *"The voice of him that crieth in the wilderness, Prepare ye the way of the LORD, make straight in the desert a highway for our God. Every valley shall be exalted, and every mountain and hill shall be made low: and the crooked shall be made straight, and the rough places plain."* Jesus levels the playing field. Everyone has the opportunity to accept or reject Him as their personal Saviour. Likewise everyone who accepts Him has the opportunity to operate in their callings and gifts. Without growing up in Him you can never rise above the valleys. You must know who you are in Christ to be "exalted" above the trials and tribulations.

There are several passages in the Bible that refer to Christians as eagles. The parallels are fascinating. Storms may depict trials just as the valleys do. An eagle can see for two miles. When he sees a storm coming, he simply uses the proceeding winds to rise above it. As we mature as Christians our 'spiritual eyesight' should improve to the point where we can discern the trials sooner and act accordingly.

In a sense these passages in Isaiah 40:3, 4, as well as Luke 1:74-80 are the nutshell version of this book. Although we should not think of ourselves more highly than we ought to, we must understand who we are in Christ. This keeps us balanced; not too low (valley), and not prideful (mountain). *"Because strait is the gate, and narrow is the way, which leadeth unto life, and few there be that find it."* (Matt 7:14) Though we live in a crooked and perverse world God wants us to be 'straight,' and live a life of integrity.

During our balancing act of highs and lows, and attempting the 'straight and narrow,' we are as diamonds in the rough. One method of polishing a diamond is to place it in a cylinder lined with sandpaper and applying water. Likewise, as we are met with circumstances that rub us the wrong way but

*Ijeabarim "ruins Of The Passers")*

apply "the washing of the water of the Word," we come forth as valuable, shiny, gems.

To incorporate Luke 1:74-80 into this analogy let's examine some key words. In verse 74 we find we have been delivered from the hand of the enemy so that we might serve God. Verse 75 says we are to do so in a holy and righteous manner. It will be more personal for you to replace the word 'child' in verse 76 with your own name and insert your spiritual gift(s) as well. Your purpose is found in verse 77; to evangelize. Because God has been merciful to us, we should show mercy. (See Matt 5:7) The mission of evangelism continues in verse 79, as we are 'the light of the world.' We must pass through the 'Valley of the shadow of death' as guided by the Holy Spirit and led by peace so that we may grow strong in the Spirit. (Verse 80)

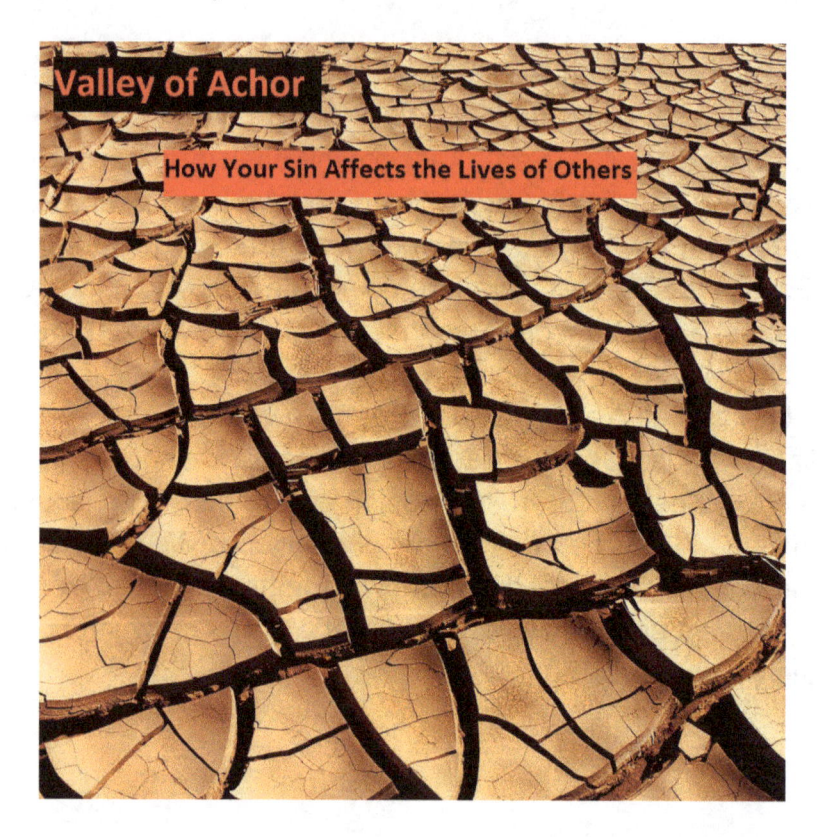

**Valley of Achor**

This valley is taken from the book of Joshua and literally means, "*Trouble.*" We begin in chapter 7, verses 1-26, "*But the children of Israel committed a trespass in the accursed thing: for Achan, the son of Carmi, the son of Zabdi, the son of Zerah, of the tribe of Judah, took of the accursed thing: and the anger of the LORD was kindled against the children of Israel. And Joshua sent men from Jericho to Ai, which is beside Bethaven, on the east of Bethel, and spake unto them, saying, Go up and view the country. And the men went up and viewed Ai. And they returned to Joshua, and said unto him, Let not all the people go up; but let about two or three thousand men go up and smite Ai; and make not all*

*Ijeabarim "ruins Of The Passers")*

*the people to labour thither; for they are but few. So there went up thither of the people about three thousand men: and they fled before the men of Ai. And the men of Ai smote of them about thirty and six men: for they chased them from before the gate even unto Shebarim, and smote them in the going down: wherefore the hearts of the people melted, and became as water. And Joshua rent his clothes, and fell to the earth upon his face before the ark of the LORD until the eventide, he and the elders of Israel, and put dust upon their heads. And Joshua said, Alas, O LORD God, wherefore hast thou at all brought this people over Jordan, to deliver us into the hand of the Amorites, to destroy us? would to God we had been content, and dwelt on the other side Jordan! And the LORD said unto Joshua, Get thee up; wherefore liest thou thus upon thy face? Israel hath sinned, and they have also transgressed my covenant which I commanded them: for they have even taken of the accursed thing, and have also stolen, and dissembled also, and they have put it even among their own stuff. Therefore the children of Israel could not stand before their enemies, but turned their backs before their enemies, because they were accursed: neither will I be with you any more, except ye destroy the accursed from among you. And Joshua, and all Israel with him, took Achan the son of Zerah, and the silver, and the garment, and the wedge of gold, and his sons, and his daughters, and his oxen, and his asses, and his sheep, and his tent, and all that he had: and they brought them unto the valley of Achor. And Joshua said, why hast thou troubled us? The LORD shall trouble thee this day. And all Israel stoned him with stones, and burned them with fire, after they had stoned them with stones. And they raised over him a great heap of stones unto this day. So the LORD turned from the fierceness of his anger. Wherefore the name of that place was called, the valley of Achor, unto this day."*

As with any valley sin produces death. Failing to deal with the sin prolongs the trial and causes separation between you and God until the issue is resolved. What I want to emphasize in this valley is the fact that sin not only caused the transgressor to lose his life, but also his entire family and the lives of 36 innocent men. Sin in the camp affects the entire body of Christ.

I can relate well to this incident and its effect. Even though I was saved a week before I went to prison, my crime disrupted my entire family. There was the shame, the embarrassment, and inevitably the humiliation. I was in management after all, climbing the corporate ladder, in pursuit of the 'American dream;' how could I disgrace myself and my family that way?

The church needs to understand how sin has a proportional effect on the entire body of Christ. To illustrate, let's suppose you belong to a church with 100 members. Now let's suppose that a scale exists representing each members level of anointing. Don't let the premise frighten you, every believer has an anointing. That simply means that the Holy Spirit resides in you. It is also important to note that you have all the Holy Spirit you will ever have; the problem is that the Holy Spirit doesn't have all of you. This hypothetical scale represents the believer's level of obedience to the Spirit; it has nothing to do with maturity. If the scale is from 1-10 with ten being the highest, it stands to reason we are most likely to experience a move of God when we are closer to the higher end of the scale. For instance if the average level of the church is an 8, or you could say at 80% of its potential on a given Sunday, the likelihood of the manifest presence of God is greater than if it were 50%.

This illustration is just a microcosm of the worldwide body of Christ. I confess I don't have any research to support it, but my guess is that the average church member would score around a 3. Therefore the church would be a 3 as well. Obviously this is not good. We need to raise the bar if we are to impact the world the way God desires us to in these last days. It's the anointing that breaks the yoke, (Isaiah 10:27). And obedience is the key to anointing as well as relationship with God.

Don't misunderstand me; I'm not promoting a works theme. Anything God chooses to do is by His mercy and grace. Yet James does point out that, *"Faith without works is dead."* (James 2:17) My wish is to convey that if the church lived like it was supposed to Monday through Saturday, then Sundays would be much more powerful.

Another way to illustrate the anointing process is by examining the tabernacle. The tabernacle had three parts: inner court, the Holy place, and the Holy of Holies. God's house is a house of order. He drew up the blueprints and He expects us to follow them.

To enter the inner court, you first offered a sacrifice at the altar. This Old Testament ritual represents laying down our own lives. *"I beseech you therefore, brethren, by the mercies of God, that ye present your bodies a living sacrifice, holy, acceptable unto God, which is your reasonable service."* (Rom 12:1) This book is about spiritual growth, and I can assure you that without sacrificing your own life for His service, there will be little growth.

Once you're willing to lay down your own agenda, you proceed to the Holy place. Here you find a wash basin filled with water. This represents *"the washing of water by the word."* (Eph 5:26) It's the Word of God that acts as our cleansing agent. As we read, study, and meditate on God's word, we renew our minds; much like reprogramming a computer operated process. With today's technology we are able to change a program in a few moments that will alter how a production process is accomplished. Spiritually speaking, this is an ongoing process, and it involves much more than a few moments. But if you are willing to lay down your life and bathe in the Word, you will be prepared to enter the Holy of Holies.

Before entering the Holy of Holies, the High Priest would place burning incense under the veil. This created a smoke screen so God wouldn't see his sin. The incense is symbolic of the blood of Jesus. When God looks at us today, He does so through the blood of Jesus.

Now, putting all this together, imagine a church that *"enters His gates with thanksgiving and into His courts with praise."* (Ps 100:4) They have laid their own lives down, studied the Bible every day, prayed, and praised God all week. They don't have to "work it up." Their "spiritual faces" are already on. Furthermore they aren't going to attempt to skip the sacrificial altar and the water basin, and run straight to the Holy of Holies expecting to experience the manifest presence of God. You see, God is everywhere, but His presence isn't manifested everywhere. That is contingent upon us; our order, our love walk, and our hunger level.

Achor means "trouble or troubler." If we wish to stay out of trouble as an individual or as the church body, we need to understand we are the body of Christ. Jesus is coming back for a "glorious church, not having spot or wrinkle, or any such thing. (Eph 5:27) If that means we have to be perfect He is never coming back. So obviously that's not it. To see an example of what Paul was referring to, consider these verses from Jude 11 and 12. *"Woe unto them! For they have gone in the way of Cain, and ran greedily after the error of Balaam for reward, and perished in the gain saying, (disobedience/strife) of Core. These are spots..."*

Too many Christians, including leaders, are guilty of going their own way. The Bible says in Proverbs 16:9, *"Man plans*

*Ijeabarim "ruins Of The Passers")*

*his way but God directs his steps."* We are like Cain when we do our own thing and expect God to bless it. Instead we should watch for what God is doing and get in on it. If we are sensitive to the direction of the Holy Spirit we will avoid a whole lot of trouble.

Then there is the Balaam spirit. Balaam was a prophet for hire. There are still those today who use religion for profit. The church was never designed to operate its business like the secular world. The rest of the world should be mimicking us, not the other way around. Still we study our demographics, marketing, and follow the trends. What we need to follow is God's plan for our particular church.

Another popular "spirit" is that of Core. Here's that believer who feels more qualified than the pastor, the deacon, or whoever holds some position he desires. After all he has more letters after his name, or perhaps attended seminary. Sometimes their reasoning involves money or position. Whatever the rationale, politics and popularity should never replace God appointments; When God sets a man in position only God should remove them. I've never seen in the Bible where a leader was removed by a vote. Core tried it and look what happened to him.

You may think you don't have an envious, controlling, religious, or self-willed spirit. The truth is we all desire to be further along spiritually than we are. We like things to go our way and we all have preconceived ideas imbedded in our minds through hearsay, ignorance, or improper teaching. We must constantly be on guard against these spirits to steer clear of Achor.

Israel's sin separated them from God. Their "hedge" was down and they were defeated by an inferior army. Joshua, the leader and a man of faith, decides to have a pity party. But God said, "Get up, take care of the sin in the camp." Don't criticize Joshua too harshly. At some point we all fall short of faith in the valley. I've had my share of pity-parties.

They don't last long and they aren't much fun. The guests are always the same; doubt, discouragement, and depression. The 3D's, and we're not talking 3rd dimensional here, these are demonic influences. These imps are out to ruin your day, steal your joy, and rob you of your faith.

To avoid the pitfalls of Achor we must take care of sin in the camp. I don't want to get sidetracked here, but a lot could be said for church discipline, or the lack thereof. The Bible teaches us that, "the anointing breaks the yoke." Sin undermines the anointing and weakens our hedge of protection. As we demonstrated earlier with the corporate anointing illustration, sin affects more than just our personal life. Sin affects the "camp," the whole body of Christ. Christians everywhere have compromised with the world. Instead of ruling and reigning we're wishful and whining. But don't be discouraged, God always has a remnant. I believe God is raising an army that dares to believe His Word; one that is willing to, "come out from among them and be ye separate." That's the purpose of this book. Preparing the remnant for use in the Kingdom of God seems to be my calling.

God has always saved a remnant for His use. He is preparing one now through process, (the valleys.) In order for Him to trust us we must learn to trust Him. Remember Annanias and Saphira? They lied about their giving and it cost them their lives. With the anointing that will be prevalent among the remnant will come a heavy responsibility.

Another important aspect to note in this account of Israel's journey is the absence of God's counsel. At no point did it appear God was consulted for a battle plan. It is possible God would have told Joshua of the trespass beforehand if Joshua had inquired. This reminds me of the deacons debating back and forth over some trivial subject until one of them got a revelation, "let's pray about it." To which another replied, "Has it

*Ijeabarim "ruins Of The Passers")*

come to that?" I realize God gave us a brain and we should use it. However, we should never get to the point where we think we are self-sufficient. We can do all things through Christ, (the anointed one and His anointing) but without him we can do nothing. When things are going well we have a tendency to take things into our own hands. Subconsciously we are saying, "I've got it from here God." Complacency is a precarious attitude and should be avoided lest we spiral into a valley prematurely.

**When trouble does come:**
1) Never blame God; trust that he is sovereign
2) Pray for insight into the situation; what am I to learn
3) Be obedient; repent immediately if you're convicted of something that opened a door for the enemy
4) Pass the test and get promoted/ failure = one more lap around the mountain and back through the valley
5) Our choices in the valley will make us powerful or pitiful; which will you choose

Are you ready to move on? If so, you have killed a few giants in Elah, you've learned to avoid the entanglements of Sorek, and you have discovered death to the flesh is the key to rapid Christian growth in the valley of the shadow of death. As an additional motivator to avoid trouble, you have learned that you're sin may affect those closest to you in Achor.

God sees your heart. He knows your desire to do His will. So now He wants you to be fruitful. John 15: 5 says *"I am the vine ye are the branches. He that abideth in me, and I in him, the same bringeth forth much fruit."* You have arrived at Zared, which means "rich in growth." Here your Christian walk becomes evident to others. It's time to grow up, but to do so requires more valleys. So I ask again, are you ready? Let's move on.

Chapter 4

ZARED
"Rich in Growth"

# CHAPTER 4
# Zared "Rich in growth"

Once you've committed to die to the flesh at Ijeabarim, change is inevitable. People will begin to see the growth, or the fruits, of your decision to pursue Christ. When you are displaying the character of Jesus without a lot of mental exercise you have arrived in Zared. Zared is where growth becomes evident. Anyone who knew you before your conversion will recognize the transformation that has taken place.

Jesus said in John 12: 24 *"Verily, verily, I say unto you, except a corn of wheat fall into the ground and die, it abideth alone: but if it die, it bringeth forth much fruit."* In order for any plant to grow it must first develop a root system. You were rooted and grounded in Oboth; you started that dying process at Ijeabarim, now we are seeing some greenery at Zared.

Notice I said earlier, "displaying the character of Jesus without a lot of mental exercise." What I'm referring to is the sincerity of your walk. You don't have to fake love, joy, peace, longsuffering, gentleness, goodness, faith, meekness, and temperance. It is genuine. We're not talking church as usual where everyone has their spiritual masks on. I mean, when the pressure is on, the character of Jesus is coming out naturally.

In the Valley of the Shadow of Death we learned the importance of dying to the flesh. We learned it's not all about us, our needs, and our wants. In the valley of Achor we learned our sin affects the lives of others as well as ourselves. Successfully overcoming these valleys has enabled us to be fruitful and arrive at Zared. When the flesh dies the Spirit has more room to operate, and when the Spirit is in control, His fruits manifest more readily. Realizing that our sin affects the rest of the body becomes a motivator for us to remain in the Spirit and forgo the selfish desires of the flesh.

As we continue our journey towards maturity, God will give us a vision. A vision serves as another motivator to propel us towards growth and purpose. When it becomes our focal point it acts as a filter in decision making. Making decisions based on our vision will help us prioritize our life choices. Can you see the difference between this approach and the "old man," which planned everything from a carnal standpoint clouded by the filters of strongholds?

At the same time we must never forget we have an enemy who wants to thwart our every move. His job is to stunt our growth so that we are less effective witnesses. One of his primary methods to hinder the growth process is through distractions. If he can get your attention off the target (vision) he will have effectively delayed your progress towards the next level of maturity. There are many forms of distractions: relationships, careers, and hobbies are just a few examples. These distractions aren't necessarily bad themselves, they simply obstruct our vision. Your eyes become focused on whatever it is you're looking at, even if your life is passing you by in the background.

Our focal point for the next two valleys will be; 1) vision and 2) distractions. In order to continue our journey to Pisgah we must move on. Serious minded Christians have learned to never rest upon their laurels. Complacency is another growth stealer. We must seek God for His vision for our lives and avoid distractions. We will discuss these principles in the next two valleys; The valley of Vision and The valley of Ono.

*Zared "rich In Growth"*

**Valley of Vision** "*Without a vision the people perish*"

**Valley of Vision** *"Where there is no vision the people perish"*

Every church and every Christian should have a vision. A vision is simply a goal or a purpose that serves as a filter in our decision making and inspires us to further the Kingdom of God. An Olympic athlete is a good example of an individual with a vision. They live a radical lifestyle geared around a training regimen that is geared to catapult them to a gold medal. The vision of that gold medal being placed around their neck drives them to train hard, sleep properly, maintain a good diet, and influences every decision of their life.

God told me through a dream over 15 years ago that I would travel the world and speak to thousands at a time, seeing many come to the saving knowledge of Jesus Christ. At first I simply dismissed it as a dream, not believing the possibility. Over the next few months I experienced something that altered my first impression and my beliefs. Three complete strangers, at separate times, prophesied to me, almost

*Nahaliel The Valley of God*

verbatim, a vision they saw for my life. It was identical to my dream. I now accept God's plan for my life as a fact.

While the vision serves as a motivator and a primary filter in decision making, I realize I have a ways to go. God is still pruning me and preparing the platform from which to launch. Perhaps this book becomes the tool that catapults me into full time ministry. Only God knows. In the meantime I must focus on: my personal relationship with Him, spiritual growth, and obedience.

Perhaps you're familiar with Paul's conversion on Damascus road. He asked Jesus, *"What would You have me do?"* Jesus didn't say, "Start five churches and for doing so you will be beaten, stoned, shipwrecked, and imprisoned." Instead Jesus said, *"arise and go into the city, it shall be told thee what thou must do."* (Acts 9:6) God wants us to see our vision clearly, but He doesn't give us a timetable and a map. If He told us of all the obstacles we would face beforehand, most of us would remain in Oboth, and many do. Until we learn to triumph in the valleys, we will not be ready to realize our vision.

> Our text for this valley comes from Isaiah 22. In verses one and two we see riotous living and mayhem. *"¹The burden of the valley of vision. What aileth thee now, that thou art wholly gone up to the housetops? ²Thou that art full of stirs, a tumultuous city, joyous city: thy slain men are not slain with the sword, nor dead in battle."* These verses along with verses 5-7 reveal a lifestyle that had opened the door for the enemy. *" ⁵For it is a day of trouble, and of treading down, and of perplexity by the Lord GOD of hosts in the valley of vision, breaking*

*Zared "rich In Growth"*

*down the walls, and of crying to the mountains. ⁶And Elam bare the quiver with chariots of men and horsemen, and Kir uncovered the shield. ⁷And it shall come to pass, that thy choicest valleys shall be full of chariots, and the horsemen shall set themselves in array at the gate."* Verse 11 depicts the action most of us take whenever we're confronted with a problem, we attempt to "fix" it ourselves. *¹¹"Ye made also a ditch between the two walls for the water of the old pool: but ye have not looked unto the maker thereof, neither had respect unto him that fashioned it long ago".*

Israel had quit trusting God, and like so many of us, relied on their own wisdom. According to Proverbs 14:12, *"There is a way which seemeth right unto a man, but the end thereof are the ways of death."* God did equip us with a brain and we should be inclined to use it. But if that is all we rely on, after we are born again, then we are wasting a valuable resource, the Holy Spirit. Proverbs 3:5,6 instructs us, *"⁵Trust in the LORD with all thine heart; and lean not unto thine own understanding. ⁶In all thy ways acknowledge Him and He shall direct thy paths."* Learning to trust the Lord for guidance is paramount to fulfilling the vision He has for your life.

Their second mistake is found in verses 12 and 13. *"And in that day did the Lord GOD of hosts call to weeping, and to mourning, and to baldness, and to girding with sackcloth: And behold joy and gladness, slaying oxen, and killing sheep, eating flesh, and drinking wine: let us eat and drink; for tomorrow we shall die."* God calls for repentance but they choose to throw a party. Responding to instructions from God by appeasing the flesh is never a good idea. We may not think of it consciously as such, but we often demonstrate the same attitude; *"let us eat and drink; for tomorrow we shall die."* Anyone conducting their life this way is deceived. The Bible says, *"It is appointed unto men once to die and after this the judgment."* (Heb 9:27) Also we find, *"The wages of sin is death"* in Romans 6:23. In essence there will be a payday someday for everyone. Accepting or rejecting Jesus Christ as your Lord and Savior determines your reward.

God has a plan and a purpose for us all. Ignoring the facts doesn't change them. Rejecting the truth doesn't alter it and choosing a lifestyle based on faulty premises will not deter our eternal destination. The truth is we are all eternal creatures and it's our choice where we spend that eternity. *"The Lord is not slack concerning his promise, as some men count slackness; but is longsuffering to us-ward, not willing that any should perish, but that all should come to repentance." But the day of the Lord will come as a thief in the night; in the which the heavens shall pass away with a great noise, and the elements shall melt with fervent heat, the earth also and the works that are therein shall be burned up. Seeing then that all these things shall be dissolved, what manner of persons ought ye to be in all holy conversation and godliness."* (2 Peter 3:9-11) God never intended for man to reside in hell but He will allow it if you so choose. Opting for a lifestyle that caters to the flesh, as Israel did here, will end with devastating consequences.

## The proper way to deal with this valley is:

1) Receive the vision (Ask God for His plan for your life)
2) Take one step at a time as you're led by the Holy Spirit (You can't make it happen)

*Zared "rich In Growth"*

3) Be patient/trust God (He never shows you all the details or the entire process at once)
4) Be faithful where you're at and you will enjoy the trip
5) Be alert to avoid wrong mindsets (Focus on victory/focus on Him)

Let's examine a few Biblical characters who fulfilled their destiny with these five principles in mind.

Noah built an ark to escape a flood. At that time no one had even seen rain.

He preached for 120 years, through mockery and scorn, while building the ark. His vision sustained him, thus saving his family as well as the human race.

Abraham believed God and had a son with Sarah well past the normal age of childbearing. When God tested him Abraham proved willing to sacrifice Isaac, his most valued treasure. How could any sane person burn their child at the stake? Because he had a vision that God would raise Isaac from the dead if necessary.

Joseph prevailed in prison because he had a vision from God at an early age. By maintaining a good attitude in spite of all the wrongdoing towards him Joseph became the Prince of Egypt. His integrity saved the nation of Israel. Esther did the same in like manner.

The best example of commitment to a vision, however, is Jesus, *"who for the joy that was set before him endured the cross, despising the shame, and is set down at the right hand of the throne of God."* Isaiah 50:5-7 confirms the resolve Jesus had for His mission, " *[5]The Lord GOD hath opened mine ear, and I was not rebellious, neither turned away back. [6]I gave my back to the smiters, and my cheeks to them that plucked off the hair: I hid not my face from shame and spitting. [7]For the Lord GOD will help me; therefore shall I not be confounded: therefore have I set my face like a flint, and*

*I know that I shall not be ashamed."* Jesus loved us so much that He allowed His own creation to mock Him, spit on Him, then crucify Him on a hill that He created. His vision for us inspired Him to endure the unimaginable.

Each of these accounts has a common theme. Without a vision the people of God, the nation of Israel, would have perished. Ergo none of us would be saved. We all need a vision to act as a catalyst in our spiritual growth process. When the valley seems never ending, the enemy is on every side, and God is nowhere to be found, your vision will sustain you. That is why Solomon was inspired to write, *"Where there is no vision the people perish."* It is that hope for a better tomorrow that propels us forward to see our faith end in sight. Then we can relate to Paul's sentiment *"I have fought a good fight, I have finished my course, I have kept the faith: Henceforth there is laid up for me a crown of righteousness, which the Lord, the righteous judge, shall give me at that day: and not to me only, but unto all them also that love his appearing.* (2 Tim 4:7,8)

*"Where there is no vision, the people perish: but he that keepeth the law, happy is he."* For years I read Proverbs 29:18 without considering the correlation between part "A" and part "B". How does "keeping the law" make us happy? How does, "keeping the law" tie in with our vision? We will explore this concept in more detail as we go along but basically we must learn to submit. We all inherit the Adamic nature when we are born; we are stubborn, rebellious, and prefer our independence to submission. Unless we learn to humble ourselves, deny the flesh, and submit to God, we will never fulfill our destiny in the Kingdom of God.

Your vision may be clear but without obedience along the way, obstacles will persist. God doesn't keep you from advancing, you do. Submitting to the Word of God is a lifelong journey and too complex to elaborate in this venue, so put a *"selah"* (pause and meditate) on that for now. Obedience to the Holy Spirit is another aspect of, "keeping the law;" Again, something that takes a lot of practice. The key to obeying the Spirit is hearing Him to start with. Our flesh is usually screaming so loud we fail to recognize when the Spirit is prompting us. Dying to the flesh is the primary focus of the valleys.

Suppose you have a vision and you are hearing the Spirit, what now? This is where the real fun starts, submission and obedience. Submission and obedience include, but is not limited to, Pastors, supervisors, and the government. For most Christians, the test will be with God and His Word. I believe most of us realize God's way is the best choice when we are making decisions. Our problem is we don't like the way God does it or the time it takes, or who is involved, etc., etc.

Isaiah prophesied of Jesus, *"The Lord GOD hath opened mine ear, and I was not rebellious, neither turned away back."* Paul commends the example of Jesus and encourages us to emulate it in Philippians 4:5-8. *"Let this mind be in you, which was also in Christ Jesus: Who, being in the form of God, thought it not robbery to be equal with God: But made himself of no reputation, and took upon him the form of a servant, and was made in the likeness of men: And being found in fashion as a man, he humbled himself, and became obedient unto death, even the death of the cross."* The Bible says we can have the mind of Christ. It also teaches us the same Spirit that raised Jesus from the dead lives in us. That being said, I believe we can all realize the vision He has entrusted us with.

Don't be discouraged if your level of obedience isn't unto death. Hebrews 5:8,9 says *"Though he were a Son, yet learned he obedience by the things which he suffered; And being made perfect, he became the author of eternal salvation unto all them that obey him."* Jesus endured process and so will we. Our obedience may never require physical death but it will definitely involve death to our flesh. As we learn obedience we will discover our anointing increases.

From our key text in Isaiah 22 we saw that Israel once again disobeyed God. Thus they were taken into captivity. God's principles are demonstrated very simply here; obey and the anointing increases. Disobey and the door is opened for the enemy. The time is at hand where we must become radically obedient if we want to be a part of the remnant that God uses mightily in the end times. The anointing breaks the yoke, disobedience invites bondage. Therefore it is wise to be obedient and when you fail, be quick to repent.

Our actions and reactions in this valley determine our destiny and the timing of its fulfillment. Stay focused on your vision. Every decision you make should be weighed accordingly. Remember it is your responsibility as to whether you realize the manifestation of your vision or not. And even though ultimately it is in His timing, you're willingness to submit is the primary factor in bringing your vision to fruition.

*Zared "rich In Growth"*

**Valley of Ono** (Stronghold of distraction)

The Hebrew word "Ono" comes from a root word that means, "To exert oneself, usually for naught." It carries the sense of great effort and strength with results that are futile. In the valley of Ono the enemy wants to distract you from your work, your vision, and or your purpose. We will look at three methods the enemy uses to distract you in order to hinder your work.

Our key text comes from Nehemiah, chapter 6. Let's examine the first four verses, *"Now it happened when Sanballat, Tobiah, Geshem the Arab, and the rest of our enemies heard that I had rebuilt the wall, and that there were no breaks left in it (though at that time I had not hung the doors in the gates), ² that Sanballat and Geshem sent to me, saying, "Come, let us meet together among the villages in the plain of Ono." But they thought to do me harm.*

*Nahaliel The Valley of God*

*³ So I sent messengers to them, saying, "I am doing a great work, so that I cannot come down. Why should the work cease while I leave it and go down to you?"*
*⁴ But they sent me this message four times, and I answered them in the same manner."* God had given Nehemiah a vision to rebuild the walls around Jerusalem. He found, as will you, anytime you set out to do a work for God the opposition comes.

John 10:10 tells us, *"The thief does not come except to steal, and to kill, and to destroy."* His initial temptation was to get Nehemiah out of position. Expect a similar approach while you're going through this valley. If he can keep you from the Word, prayer, or ministering in your gifts and calling, he will have effectually distracted you from your "great work." A "great work" is a relative term. It depends upon where you are in your walk and could range from helping out in the nursery or going to the mission field. Regardless of the task, if it's for God, there will be opposition.

The second half of John 10:10 says, *"I am come that they might have life and that they might have it more abundantly."* Developing a proper relationship with God through prayer and the Word will keep you focused on others, (ministry) and help you avoid distraction. Notice verse two of Nehemiah 6, *"they thought to do me mischief."* Because Nehemiah was in right relationship with God he had discernment. He knew the intentions of the enemy. We should never be so conscience of the enemy that we lose sight of Jesus but we must maintain our awareness that the enemy exists and wants to destroy us. Balance, balance, balance...

The word *abundantly* in John 10:10 means, "beyond measure" in the Greek. Jesus wants to bless you Spirit, soul, and body, financially, and socially. This valley will determine if you are able to receive it. Staying focused on your vision is vital to your calling and your personal growth. If satan can distract you he will gain ground into your life and hinder the great work God has called you to.

Now let's examine verses 5 – 9, *"Then sent Sanballat his servant unto me in like manner the fifth time with an open letter in his hand; Wherein was written, It is reported among the heathen, and Gashmu saith it, that thou and the Jews think to rebel: for which cause thou buildest the wall, that thou mayest be their king, according to these words. And thou hast also appointed prophets to preach of thee at Jerusalem, saying, there is a king in Judah: and now shall it be reported to the king according to these words. Come now therefore, and let us take counsel together. Then I sent unto him, saying, There are no such things done as thou sayest, but thou feignest them out of thine own heart.*

*For they all made us afraid, saying, their hands shall be weakened from the work, that it be not done. Now therefore, O God, strengthen my hands."* If the enemy can't steer you off course, he will attempt to ruin your testimony through rumors, lies, and confusion.

One trick of the devil is to push the "buttons" that he has placed in you himself over the years, (strongholds) to extract a response from you that is out of character with Christ. I've never done much fishing but I do know that different types of fish require different types of bait. Some are caught with live bait and others are captured easier with lures. And if the fish aren't responding the fisherman will either try another spot or another lure. The devil is persistent. He will try different lures and different methods to distract you. Don't take the bait or satan will reel you in.

Our response should mimic that of Jesus whom the Word says, *"Opened not His mouth."* He sought no glory for Himself and was not trapped into proving anything to His accusers. Philippians 2:7,8 tells us, *"But made himself of no reputation, and took upon him the form of a servant, and was made in the likeness of men: And being found in fashion as a man, he humbled himself, and became obedient unto death, even the death of the cross."* We must never intentionally alienate others but at the same time must learn to honor God, not our reputation. Be a God pleaser, not a people pleaser or you will find yourself in Ono. To be in Ono is to exert yourself, (works) particularly to please others, and usually for naught. Allow God to deal with your accusers and focus on the task at hand. *"No weapon that is formed against thee shall prosper; and every tongue that shall rise against thee in judgment thou shalt condemn. This is the heritage of the servants of the LORD, and their righteousness is of me, saith the LORD."*

Growing up I had always dreamed of owning a Porsche. I loved the body style of the 944. In 1994 my opportunity came and I purchased a red 1984 Porsche 944. It was in pretty good condition but I began restoring and customizing it immediately. New paint, ground effects, custom lighting, interior work, and of course wheels. By the time I was through I'd spent twice as much fixing it up as I had paid for it. A friend of mine informed me that it had become my "Ishmael" because it wasn't God's plan, it was my own. This was an Ono and it cost me, cash, credit card debt, and two speeding tickets.

Then to tie in with my second point, rumors began at my workplace that I was selling drugs to supplement my income. At least I did pass that test. I didn't attempt to defend myself or try to figure out who had fabricated the story. I simply laughed it off and eventually it went away. When others recognize that you are sincere about your Christian walk they tend to react in one of two ways when it comes to rumors: 1) they will disregard it because it is inconsistent with what they perceive of you, or 2) they will spread and perhaps even embellish the tale because it eases their conscience about their own sin.

Another principle to employ in this situation was demonstrated by the apostles in Acts chapter 4. Verses 29-31 say, *"And now, Lord, behold their threatenings: and grant unto thy servants, that with all boldness they may speak thy word, By stretching forth thine hand to heal; and that signs and wonders may be done by the name of thy holy child Jesus. And when they had prayed, the place was shaken where they were assembled together; and they were all filled with the Holy Ghost, and they spake the word of God with boldness."* Praying for more boldness instead of adopting the victim mentality apparently pleases God. He shook the place like He had at Pentecost and again later when He freed Paul and Silas from prison. Praising God during the storm releases His power to manifest in your situation whereas cowering down to the enemy will invite captivity.

Now let's examine verses 10 – 13. *"Afterward I came unto the house of Shemaiah the son of Delaiah the son of Mehetabeel, who was shut up; and he said, Let us meet together in the house of God, within the temple, and let us shut the doors of the temple: for they will come to slay thee; yea, in the night will they come to slay thee. And I said, Should such a man as I flee? and who is there, that, being as I am, would go into the temple to save his life? I will not go in. And, lo, I perceived that God had not sent him; but that he pronounced this prophecy against me: for Tobiah and Sanballat had hired him. Therefore was he hired, that I should be afraid, and do so, and sin, and that they might have matter for an evil report, that they might reproach me."*

The third distraction used by the enemy here was fear. Fear is the opposite of faith. Romans 14:28 tells us,

*Nahaliel The Valley of God*

*"Whatsoever is not of faith is sin."* (2 Tim 1:7) Fear is a sin and comes from the enemy. It is a ploy intended to distract you from your purpose in life. When you walk in fear you are essentially allowing the enemy to accomplish his mission: kill, steal, and destroy. Once you give into the fear he tempts you with, he immediately publishes an "evil report" against you. Revelation 12:10 names him, "the accuser of the brethren."

We should have no fear. Romans 8:31 tells us, *"If God be for us, who can be against us." "God has not given us the spirit of fear but of love, power, and a sound mind."* The Word also tells us in 1 John 4:18, *"There is no fear in love; but perfect love casteth out fear: because fear hath torment. He that feareth is not made perfect in love."* The word perfect here means mature. As our relationship with God is developed we learn to love Him more which in turn builds our faith and decreases our fear. God, the creator of the universe, is still on the throne and still in control. James 4:7 encourages us to, *"Submit yourselves therefore to God. Resist the devil, and he will flee from you."* When we focus on our relationship with God, He will give us a game plan: to defeat the enemy, eliminate fear, and avoid "Ono."

Making decisions based on fear is like bringing a knife to a gunfight, you will lose every time. We must learn to depend on the Lord for leadership while we're in the valleys. Acting in our own wisdom is futile, it becomes an Ono. By submitting ourselves to God we resist the devil instead of assisting the devil. The devil has no power except what we give him. When we act in faith, based on the Word and direction of the Holy Spirit, we are assisting God and His Kingdom. By acting in fear, we come into agreement with the devil and the powers of darkness.

*"So the wall was finished in the twenty and fifth day of the month Elul, in fifty and two days. And it came to pass,*

*that when all our enemies heard thereof, and all the heathen that were about us saw these things, they were much cast down in their own eyes: for they perceived that this work was wrought of our God."* (Neh 6:15,16) Maintaining focus on God and the vision He has given you will sustain you in the valleys that come with the pursuit of His Kingdom. The apostles exhorted the early church in Acts 14:22, *"continue in the faith...we must through much tribulation enter the Kingdom of God."*

Distractions come in many forms: TV, computers, hobbies, work, relationships, etc., etc. Anything that steals your time from God and/or the vision He has given you can become an Ono. Nehemiah finished the wall. He refused to allow the enemy to distract him from his purpose and destiny. Failure was not an option. If you apply this attitude to your valley success is inevitable and God is glorified.

## Chapter 5

## Arnon "Radical Stream"

CHAPTER 5

# Arnon "Radical Stream"

---

The Hebrew word Arnon means, "radical stream" but the root word means, "To shout or cry out for joy." Contextually Arnon is a picture of a young Christian who is maturing into a radical believer. This is a believer who is not ashamed of the Gospel. One who is walking the walk and not just talking the talk. I'm not talking obnoxious here, but someone who is real wherever they're at. They have genuine joy and it's obvious they have been saved. *"Now when they saw the boldness of Peter and John, and perceived that they were unlearned and ignorant men, they marvelled; and they took knowledge of them, that they had been with Jesus."* (Acts 4:13) That's what I'm talking about!

I worked with a fellow believer once that exemplified this lifestyle. Every time you saw him in the plant he would throw both arms up in the air and praise the Lord. He didn't do this to draw attention to himself, he didn't notice or care who was around. He was simply praising God and encouraging you to do the same.

You may not have a personality that enjoys this type of exuberance. The issue here is not how you choose to express your love for God, but rather how radical you choose to live for Him. If you are embarrassed at what God leads you to do you are probably not ready for Arnon. I can assure you God will test your obedience with some pretty strange promptings at times.

When you do step out in obedience He will reward you with more and more **stability** (valley #1). At the same time **contention and opposition** (valley #2) are just around the corner. You must grow in strength in order to hold your ground when the trials and persecution come. You will never please God being a man-pleaser. Remember it was the religious crowds that hated Jesus. They opposed Him at every turn. So don't expect everyone to commend you for having a heart for God, even among fellow Christians. If you're too radical it brings conviction upon their lives. On the other hand, know this; you'll be in good company. Jesus was a radical.

The first valley we will discuss in this segment is the "valley of preparation." We have established our foundation, but we must remain stable as we train to reign. Without stability we will falter when the opposition arises. In this chapter, we will learn how to stand without taking offence when we come under attack for our radical lifestyle. When we emerge victorious we will shout for joy because "the joy of the Lord is our strength." Halleluiah!

*Arnon "radical Stream"*

**Valley of Preparation**
Stability through His Strength

## **Valley of Preparation** – stability through
His strength

Do you believe God has a sense of humor? Well, He does. He chose this day for me to write about this valley. A day when I feel I was tested and failed. Am I a hypocrite? I don't think so. I just realized once again I am human. This valley is about stability through *His* strength, not our own. No matter how much you're prepared, no matter how stable you become, days like this will happen.

We had a special mid-week service this week. Several churches attended about a three hour service with two very special international speakers. It was wonderful except for the fact I got to bed very late. Still in the morning I felt fine. I arrived at work early as I usually do and headed for my "prayer closet." A term my co-workers and I used when referring to the part of the plant we used to pray before work each morning. I waited for my prayer partners to arrive and join me, all was well.

Afterwards, I saddled my donkey, one of the nicknames for a forklift. I was a material handler in the automotive industry

*Nahaliel The Valley of God*

at that time. Immediately, I noticed things were in disarray. I wasn't too happy about that and gave into murmuring and complaining. I knew better and attempted to limit my griping only to a preacher and a deacon who work in the same area as I. After all, they are spiritual people, they would understand . . . right? Wrong! God doesn't like murmuring and complaining, just ask Israel about her forty years in the desert.

It's an hour and half later, I'm just now catching up. My attitude is improving, but I'm still rushing. I pick up a basket of parts to take to the job, but one falls out. Normally, I would stop, inspect the part, and determine its disposition; but not today. I'm in rush mode. I'll just run over it, pick it up later, and scrap it. I'm a performance oriented person, but usually my integrity comes first. Not today, not this morning anyway, and I paid for it.

The part went under my fork truck and punctured a hole in the transmission filter. Needless to say, my vehicle was out of commission. I felt helpless as my poor little donkey sat idle, "bleeding to death." Now I would have to use another fork truck, one that looked just like mine, but with completely different characteristics. To make matters worse, when I finally did get off my donkey, I was standing in transmission fluid. I picked up the ruined part, bathed in the red oily substance, without gloves and quickly discarded it. I proceeded to apprise my group-leader of the situation and headed to the men's room to wash my hands. There, to add insult to injury, I discovered there were no paper towels. It was going to be a long day.

I realize my "trauma" is trivial compared to the hunger in third world countries, the unrest of the Middle East, or the aftermath of the numerous disasters the world has experienced of late. Nevertheless it's real to me; it's my life at the moment, and trials vary in relevance from believer to believer.

What may seem a mere inconvenience to one person might appear traumatic to another. It comes down to the perspective of the moment. The perspective is influenced by factors such as personality, environment, timing and maturity.

Our goal is to pass the test through preparation, become more stable, and learn to depend on His strength. *"The spirit indeed is willing but the flesh is weak."* (Matt 26:41) To prepare means, "To get ready beforehand." I don't wake up Sunday mornings and debate with myself as to whether or not I'm going to church. I've predetermined this, it's not an option. Folks if you don't prepare you will be left behind. I don't mean you will lose your salvation; you just will never reach your full potential spiritually. That is the main purpose of this book, to help you be all you can be for the Master.

Stable, "To be firmly established or steady in purpose. Durable." We become firmly established by being rooted and grounded in the Word. As we mature we become more consistent in our walk and our endurance for the trials is greater. We come to realize our training is for a marathon, not a sprint. Becoming more stable enables us to be used for His purpose to a greater degree.

The Valley of Preparation is a transition point. It's where we begin training for reigning. We must prepare ourselves for success. We must pray believing and act on faith, not wishes and doubts. *"A double minded man is unstable in all his ways."* (James 1:8) Our mission is to prepare ourselves for His use and His glory by becoming stable, positioning ourselves to fulfill His purpose for our lives.

> *"The voice of him that crieth in the wilderness, Prepare ye the way of the* Lord, *make straight in the desert a highway for our God.*

> *⁴ Every valley shall be exalted, and every mountain and hill shall be made low: and the crooked shall be made straight, and the rough places plain:"*

In these verses Isaiah got a glimpse of John the Baptist preparing the way for the first coming of Jesus. The glory of the Lord was revealed in spectacular fashion through the ministry of Jesus. He is *"The fullness of the Godhead bodily,"* He was *"Emanuel, God with us,"* and He will be *"The Faithful and True...The Word of God...The King of Kings and Lord of Lords"* that returns upon a white horse with His armies to rule and reign. (Rev 19) *"I am Alpha and Omega, the beginning and the ending, saith the Lord, which is, and which was, and which is to come, the Almighty."* (Rev 1:8)

Imagine the creator of the universe, the God that measured all the water on earth in one hand and all the mountains in the other, confining Himself to human form. He loves us that much! And there's more; He died on the cross to pay our sin debt so that we might have eternal life.

Jesus leveled the playing field. He is an equal opportunity Savior. Our responsibility as believers is to insure that everyone is aware of that opportunity. That is what John the Baptist did to prepare for the first coming and that is what we must do to prepare for the second coming. We must prepare, (get ready) as individuals and as a church; Get things straight, remove the rough places, level the mountains, and conquer the valleys. Stability is a must. As we cooperate with Him He will give us the strength to endure the process that prepares us for use in the Kingdom. We are training for reigning. So get ready.

Each of the following four factors represents an obstacle. These obstacles hinder our ability to advance the Kingdom.

Do we have to be perfect? No! David wasn't perfect, yet God used him in a great way. He was a man after God's own heart. Only Jesus was perfect. Our responsibility is to cooperate with the Holy Spirit as He directs to remove the obstacles in our lives. God will give us grace and mercy for the rest. Is that presumptuous? Again, no. He did so with everyone He used to accomplish His purpose in the scriptures, and continues to do so today.

**Valleys** As stated, valleys represent trials, and it's in the trials that we discover our weaknesses. God knows our weaknesses. He wants us to realize what they are and then overcome them. Most of us are happy when everything is going our way. It's when the pressure is on that we see our real character. The Bible teaches us that the joy of the Lord is our strength. The devil wants to steal your joy so you will become weak and therefore more susceptible to his temptations. *"If thou faint in the day of adversity, thy strength is small."* (Prov 24:10) Your strength is small when your joy is small.

At some point we all must realize the difference between joy and happiness. Happiness is based on circumstances; joy is a fruit of the Spirit. Walking in the Spirit allows you to retain your joy regardless of your circumstances. When the disciples were beaten for preaching the Gospel they rejoiced that they were counted worthy to suffer for His name. (Acts 5:41) Paul and Silas praised Him at midnight after being beaten and imprisoned and were freed, igniting a city wide revival. (Acts 16) Joy is a powerful force. Romans 14:17 tells us *"For the kingdom of God is not meat and drink; but righteousness, and peace, and joy in the Holy Ghost."*

We all get discouraged from time to time when things don't go our way or we want something we can't have. The Kingdom of God is not about things, it's about relationship. If our relationship is right we will have peace and joy in spite of our circumstances. Paul said *"I have learned, in whatsoever state I am, therewith to be content."* If we strive for that type of attitude then God will supply our needs as well. *"But seek ye first the kingdom of God, and his righteousness; and all these things shall be added unto you."*

It's in the valleys that we should seek God more earnestly. It is His Spirit that reveals the mountains, the crooked places, and the rough edges He desires to alleviate from our lives. Remember, nothing is too hard for God. He parted the Red Sea, made time standstill, and caused a donkey to talk. He can handle whatever problem areas exist in your life.

**Mountains:** A mountain is anything in us that exalts itself. *"Casting down imaginations, and every high thing that exalteth itself against the knowledge of God, and bringing into captivity every thought to the obedience of Christ;"* (2 Cor 10:5) Within this verse lies a tall order. It says we need to control our imagination; reject everything that doesn't line up with the Word and capture every thought that isn't Christ like.

You may recall in our first set of valleys we discussed how the thought process is directly linked to what we speak. A believer who doesn't submit their mind to renewal through the Word will speak things they shouldn't. When you allow words to come out of your mouth that aren't scriptural you are opening yourself up to demonic agreement. Remember the enemy has no power except what you give him.

Jesus said *"Cleanse first that which is within the cup and platter, that the outside of them may be clean also."* (Matt 23:26) By keeping our thoughts in check on a consistent basis with the Word of God, we are renewing our mind. We are receiving *"the washing of water by the Word."* (Eph 5:26) We are becoming purified from the inside out. Proverbs 4:23 tells us *"Keep thy heart with all diligence; for out of it are the issues of life."* We must guard our minds, it is the only entrance satan has. Philippians 4:8 is our example of the idea thought life, *"Whatsoever things are true, whatsoever things are honest, whatsoever things are just, whatsoever things are pure, whatsoever things are lovely, whatsoever things are of good report; if there be any virtue, and if there be any praise, think on these things."* The verses just prior to this tell us how to do that, *"Be anxious for nothing, but in everything by prayer and supplication, with thanksgiving, let your requests be made known to God; and the peace of God, which surpasses all understanding, will guard your hearts and minds through Christ Jesus."*

Pride was satan's downfall; don't let it be yours. Pride is the number one issue when referring to mountains in the context we are discussing here. Proverbs 16:18 warns, *"Pride goes before destruction, and a haughty spirit before a fall."* Peter tells us in 1Peter 5:5 *"...God resisteth the proud, and giveth grace to the humble."* According to the Strong's concordance grace is defined as "the divine influence upon the heart, and its reflection in the life." The power of God working *in* me appeals to me more than God resisting me. Jesus said in Matthew 23:12 *"Whosoever exalts himself shall be abased; and he that humbles himself shall be exalted.* "Beware of the mountains in your life. We must become well balanced Christians in order to prepare the way for the second coming of Christ.

**Crooked**: When I think of a "crooked" person, I think of a con artist or a thief. Maybe you don't run scams on others or steal, but do you keep your word? Do you do things right, even when no one is looking? Do you pay your tithes and taxes honestly? Even if you do chances are you still have "crooked places" in your life. I think of integrity as the opposite of crooked. Do you practice integrity?

Many Christians I know lack integrity in one or more areas of their life. Some pay tithes on their net instead of their gross. God said first fruits. Some buy pirated DVD's, that's illegal. Others rob their employers by not doing their jobs. Colossians 3:22, 23 tell me Christians should be the best workers, not the slackers. And what about all of us who feel it's ok to drive 5 mph above the speed limit? I could go on until I hit everyone with something; none of us are perfect. Nevertheless we should strive towards the mark. Our actions speak louder than our words and make no mistake the world is watching. More importantly God is watching. Not to condemn, but to find someone He can trust; someone He can use.

Integrity is an important characteristic to me, but it's even more important to God. He said *"Be ye Holy for I am Holy,"* (1 Peter 1:16) and *"Man looks on the outward appearance but God looks on the heart."* (1 Sam 16:7) He searches our hearts and He knows our motives. You can't fool God; He knows your every thought. 1 Corinthians 11:31 says *"If we would judge ourselves we would not be judged."* Watch your motives; they are vital to maintaining integrity. When God sees you are ready for the next level He will promote you. Until then continue through the valley of preparation.

**Rough Places:** Diamonds are one of nature's most precious commodities. It takes immense pressure and a significant amount of time to form a diamond. We are all diamonds in the rough. We are valuable to God but must allow Him to form us through process over time. Each of us has rough places in our lives; character flaws that hinder our effectiveness for the kingdom.

Diamonds are graded as much by their flaws as their size. God is not grading us by our external attributes either. The fewer the flaws the more valuable the diamond is; the more valuable we are to the kingdom. I'm not talking about perfection, I'm referring to character. Do you want to grow? I believe you do or you wouldn't have read this far. So *"press towards the high calling of God in Christ Jesus."* Amen!

The more stable we become in the valleys, mountains, crooked, and rough places, the more prepared we are for His use. I've said a lot about these two verses in Isaiah 40 and could say more but we need to move on. Look at verse five, *"And the glory of the LORD shall be revealed, and all flesh shall see it together: for the mouth of the LORD hath spoken it."* The Lord will not share His Glory with flesh, which is why we must die to ours. He wants to use us in the Spirit to manifest His works on the earth that the lost might see their need. Will you become a willing vessel?

*"For I reckon that the sufferings of this present time are not worthy to be compared with the glory which shall be revealed in us."* (Rom 8:18) As you go through the Valley of Preparation, as with most valleys, there will be some suffering of the flesh. Just think of it as more garbage to be left at Ijeabarim. What you gain will be far superior to what you are leaving behind. Isaiah said it is not even worthy to compare. Paul stated it like this, *"For our light affliction, which is but for a moment, worketh for us a far more exceeding and eternal weight of glory;"* (2Cor 4:17) Listen to what Paul called *light* affliction from 2 Corinthians 11:24-28. *"Of the Jews five times received I forty stripes save one. Thrice was I beaten with rods, once was I stoned, thrice I suffered shipwreck, a night and a day I have been in the deep; In journeyings often, in perils of waters, in perils of robbers, in perils by mine own countrymen, in perils by the heathen, in perils in the city, in perils in the wilderness, in perils in the sea, in perils among false brethren; In weariness and painfulness, in watchings often, in hunger and thirst, in fastings often, in cold and*

*nakedness. Beside those things that are without, that which cometh upon me daily, the care of all the churches."*

Most Christians today feel like they are under a great spiritual attack if they have a flat tire, a runny nose, or someone mistreats them in the slightest. God forbid if all that happened in one day. But take heart, even if your circumstances are significantly more serious than these examples, they are "but for a moment."

> *"Hast thou not known? Hast thou not heard, that the everlasting God, the LORD, the Creator of the ends of the earth, fainteth not, neither is weary? There is no searching of his understanding. He giveth power to the faint; and to them that have no might he increaseth strength. Even the youths shall faint and be weary, and the young men shall utterly fall: But they that wait upon the LORD shall renew their strength; they shall mount up with wings as eagles; they shall run, and not be weary; and they shall walk, and not faint."* (Isaiah 40:28-31)

Notice in these verses God is saying I don't get tired and if you rely on Me neither will you. That's *my* "nutshell" version but look a little deeper. When God created the universe He wasn't wore out. He wasn't even sweating or mentally fatigued. Genesis does record that He rested on the seventh day, but it wasn't because He was tired. He was finished! Seven is God's number of completion.

*"Who hath measured the waters in the hollow of his hand, and meted out heaven with the span, and comprehended the dust of the earth in a measure, and weighed the mountains in scales, and the hills in a balance?"* (Isaiah 40:12) God is

a big God. Imagine; all the bodies of water on the earth are as a few drops in the palm of His hand. It stands to reason, regardless of our actions, we will not tax the strength of God almighty. The Valley of Preparation is about stability through **His** strength.

We must learn to draw from His strength and not our own. Sounds good, right? But is it feasible? I say yes! Why? Because the Bible says we can. Look at verse 29 again, *"He giveth power to the faint; and to them that have no might He increaseth strength."* We receive the power and the strength the same way we receive salvation, by faith. *"Not by might, nor by power but by My Spirit saith the Lord of Hosts."* (Zach 4:6) It's not our power and strength we're after. We are infinitesimal in comparison to God and to His power.

What is the key? How do we draw from His strength? The answer to both questions can be found in one word. Wait. The Hebrew word for *wait* is Quavah which means, "To bind together, to collect, or to expect." I believe what the Lord is trying to convey to us through this verse is that we can draw from His strength if:

1) We **bind** ourselves together with Him in a relationship of faith.
2) **Collect** the wisdom we glean from the Word.
3) And fully **expect** a manifestation of His power when we need to complete an assignment for Him.

Waiting is not sitting around idly wishing God would do something. To "wait upon the Lord" as rendered in verse 31 is proactive. It requires something on our part, as with all the promises of God. The Father desires relationship with His sons and daughters. He wants to fellowship with us. Our response in obedience to His bidding will often require more stamina than we can possibly muster on our own. That's when He expects us to draw from Him, depend on Him. He will always give you everything you need to carry out any task He has given you. So expect it, pray for it, and act on it. Take the "see and wait attitude" as opposed to the "wait and see" attitude.

Just a few verses away in Isaiah 41:10 God reiterates His promise with these words, *"Fear thou not; for I am with thee: be not dismayed; for I am thy God: I will strengthen thee; yea, I will help thee; yea, I will uphold thee with the right hand of my righteousness."* God is able. Can we trust Him? Those that do shall soon soar as an eagle. The passive, casual, carnal Christian will quickly faint when adversity comes. God gave us a free will. Which will you choose; eagle or chicken? Chickens are what you eat for dinner. Eagles represent freedom. You are free through His strength. Amen!

*Arnon "radical Stream"*

**Valley of Esek and Sitnah:**
(Contention and opposition)

This valley comes from Genesis 26. We will focus on several verses but to fully realize the significance of the principles being taught here I suggest reading the whole chapter. Why don't you do so now, it will acquaint you with the background of our key verses and perhaps you will discover some truths of your own. Go ahead; read the chapter, I'll wait for you…

Notice there is a famine in the land. This is the second famine recorded in the Bible. The first was with Abram where he went to Egypt and lied about his wife Sarai. There was no specific instruction given to Abram recorded in Genesis 12, but the scripture says "Abram went *down* into Egypt." Understand Abram wasn't Abraham yet, like most of us he had faith but he was still on a journey. He had left his home and most of his family behind to embark on an expedition based on a word from God. He didn't know where he was going, he was leaving behind the familiar, but he left.

Abram's faith was young so instead of going up or forward, he went down into Egypt. We've all been there. Instead of running to God or waiting on further instruction, we run our own way, to the world system, or to the familiar. When you choose this route you are going down.

Years later Isaac is in a similar situation. This time the scripture records specific instructions "Go *not* down into Egypt." As "Arnon" believers we hear from God and are obedient. As you read in verse three there are blessings in obedience. Verse twelve exhibits the blessings of God for obedience. Isaac received a hundred fold return on his crops that year. You will always be blessed for sowing in the land that God leads you to. Keep in mind that *blessing* means "to prosper." Paul said *"I wish above all things that thou mayest prosper and be in health, even as thy soul prospers."* (3 Jn 2) Blessings are not just financial. They are spirit, soul, body, socially, and financially. Wholeness.

A lie of the devil is that we have to be perfect. Consider our subject, Isaac; a deceiver from his youth. As I mentioned earlier Abram lied about his wife in the same manner as his son did. But the best example of the grace of God is David. David was far from perfect yet the Bible says David was a man after God's own heart. I'm not suggesting you live any way you choose; I am merely pointing out the need for balance. If you have a heart for God you won't adopt that attitude anyway. What I want you to understand is that when you do go down to Egypt, get back up. Don't stay there. David was a man after God's own heart because he repented. Run to God, not from Him.

Now let's turn our attention to our key verses. *"And the man waxed great, and went forward, and grew until he became very great: For he had possession of flocks, and possession of herds, and great store of servants: and the Philistines envied him. For all the wells which his father's servants had digged in the days of Abraham his father, the Philistines had stopped them, and filled them with earth."* Isaac went forward

Arnon "radical Stream"

and grew and God blessed him. As mentioned at the outset, with success comes envy. Envy stirs up strife, opposition, and contention. Paul admonished the Corinthian church in 1 Corinthians 3:3 that they were babes because of their envy, strife and divisions. These traits should not be a part of our character but we can expect it from others.

The enemy wants to stop up our wells whenever we are going forward with God. A well is anything that draws you closer to God. Whatever draws you closer to God will come under attack from the enemy. There won't be a trumpet blast or fireworks to announce his arrival. He will use friends, family, hobbies, or anything he can to distract you from your well(s).

*"And Isaac's servants digged in the valley, and found there a well of springing water. And the herdmen of Gerar did strive with Isaac's herdmen, saying, the water is ours: and he called the name of the well Esek; because they strove with him." "And they digged another well, and strove for that also: and he called the name of it Sitnah."* (Gen 26:19-21) Contention and opposition are prevalent in our everyday walk, particularly when you are attempting to draw from your "wells." When strife comes we must learn how to deal with it in a manner that is pleasing to God; one that brings Him glory. Learn to trust God in this valley. We cannot obtain Pisgah without enduring some opposition. Galatians 6:9 says *"And let us not be weary in <u>well</u> doing: for in due season we shall reap, if we faint not."*

*"And he removed from thence, and digged another well; and for that they strove not: and he called the name of it Rehoboth; and he said, For now the LORD hath made room for us, and we shall be fruitful in the land."* (vs 22) Isaac moved on in peace and came to what he named "Rehoboth." (Wide area) God has a place for every believer to grow and prosper. He desires to see His children enjoy a "wide area" with wells

that bring forth abundance. Jesus came that we might have life and that more abundantly. (Jn 10:10)

We must seek the areas that God wants us to dig. You will reap what you sow. For instance, if you dig in the Word, then the Word will come out of you. *"The mouth of a righteous man is a well of life."* (Prov 10:11) A "well", (Be-er) is where we are going next but we must start "digging" in this valley. Utilizing our wells to draw closer to God will enable us to avoid strife and put us in a position to be used of Him.

If we're to avoid offence when contention and opposition come, we must be rooted and grounded in the Word. The Word does not return void. Once it flows from our spirit we will overcome the demons of contention and opposition. Then God will bless us with our space; A wide area where we can be fruitful. The wide area represents larger parameters. As we go forward and grow we're less easily offended. The fruits of the Spirit; love, joy, peace, longsuffering, gentleness, goodness, faith, meekness and temperance become spiritual weapons. When you can walk in love in the face of opposition you are engaged in spiritual warfare. When you can retain your joy despite adversity you give the devil a headache. When you sow in peace you receive it in return. Isaac walked in these fruits and God blessed him.

At this point I trust you believe that God has a purpose for your life and I hope you know what it is. If you're at Arnon you are radical for Jesus. Having a vision and purpose are keys to maintaining your motivation. Proverbs 29:18 tells us, *"Where there is no vision the people perish."* Isaac's grandson, Joseph, had a vision and favor. It brought envy, contention, opposition, strife, and led to years of mistreatment and imprisonment. Joseph maintained his faith in God, and the vision God had given him, and eventually became the Prince of Egypt who saved Israel from famine.

James 3:16 says, *"For where envying and strife is, there is confusion and every evil work."* We must not fall prey to the bait of the enemy when he employs such tactics against us through others. By the same token, we should avoid envy, strife, and confusion ourselves. *"For God is not the author of confusion, but of peace..."*

(1 Cor 14:33) If God is not the author guess who is. Paul encourages us in Philippians 2:3 with these words *"Let nothing be done through strife or vain glory; but in lowliness of mind let each esteem others better than ourselves."* The enemy is always at work to rob you of your fruits. He interjects hate for love, depression for joy, and in this valley it's strife for peace. Don't take the bait.

Years ago I lived in an apartment complex where the issue of a parking space escalated into a shooting death. While in prison a man I knew was stabbed and killed for a can of Copenhagen. Both incidents were senseless and selfish. When our pride exceeds our common sense we incur strife over trivial issues, and as illustrated, may pay for it for the rest of our lives. Philippians 2:4-8 says *"Look not every man on his own things, but every man also on the things of others. Let this mind be in you, which was also in Christ Jesus: Who, being in the form of God, thought it not robbery to be equal with God: But made himself of no reputation, and took upon him the form of a servant, and was made in the likeness of men: And being found in fashion as a man, he humbled himself, and became obedient unto death, even the death of the cross."* If Jesus could die via the horrific means of crucifixion for no wrongdoing, can't we allow our flesh to suffer a little bit and relinquish a parking space.

Jesus is the Prince of Peace. (Is 9:6) He promised us we could have it as well in John 14:27 *"Peace I leave with you, my peace I give unto you: not as the world giveth, give I unto you. Let not your heart be troubled, neither let it be afraid."* That doesn't mean we won't have trials and tribulations; It just means we can enjoy peace in the midst of the storm if we choose to trust Him. According to our passage in Philippians serving the Father and serving others is consistent with the mind of Christ. He wasn't preoccupied with himself and his reputation.

Come to Rehoboth where your parameters of offense are broader. Don't allow yourself to be easily offended. Eleanor Roosevelt said "No one can insult you without your permission." You have a choice. It will help you to know that regardless of whom the person is, the enemy is the instigator. We must humble ourselves and die to more of our flesh. Jesus died to His flesh spiritually and literally to afford us the grace to do the same.

From Rehoboth Isaac ventured to Beer-Sheba, "well of oath." There God confirmed His covenant. I believe God will bring you to Beer-Sheba many times as you progress in your spiritual walk. He wants to reassure you with confirmation of His plan for your life. Hebrews 6:18 assures us *"It is impossible for God to lie."* God never breaks covenant, but you can. Avoid the pitfalls of contention and opposition and move on to Be-er.

**BE'ER** "A Well"  Chapter 6

# CHAPTER 6
# Be-er "Well"

---

*"Counsel in the heart of man is like deep water; but a man of understanding will draw it out"* (Proverbs 20:5)

Ah! Be-er, this is a fun place. This is where I spend most of my time. That is mostly due to the fact that I'm a Sunday school teacher. Be-er is the level of Christian maturity where we practice the art of ministering to others on a consistent basis. As we grow we develop some practical wisdom for our walk. We are in a place where we can give a drink of the Word to those in need. We have become a well of life to others as the Holy Spirit leads.

Notice I said this is where I spend most of my time. Whatever spiritual gifts God blesses you with; He gives you a zeal for it. I enjoy encouraging others in the Word. I mentioned at the outset that we all go through the valleys more than once, at different times, and to various degrees. We also experience the seven levels of maturity in a similar fashion. No matter what level of maturity you reach there will always be more to learn. So be prepared to revisit the valleys as well as the plateaus of life.

For example; everyone starts at Oboth and proceeds to Ijeabarim. Remember Ijeabarim means "ruins of the passers." It's the place of repentance, where we discard our junk. This will be a place you probably visit often. The Lord is constantly pruning and the valleys continue to expose the bad fruit that we must repent of if we expect to grow in the Lord. After Ijeabarim we come to Zared, because pruning promotes growth. A growth spurt tends to make us a little more radical, which is Arnon. Then we desire to share what we learned which brings us back to Be-er. *"Every branch that beareth fruit, He purgeth it, that it may bring forth more fruit."* (Jn 15:2)

Regardless of how far along you are as a Christian you will revisit the various levels of maturity from time to time. In fact I think you will discover that you are frequently at two or more places simultaneously. For instance God has used me while I was struggling with Goliath at Elah ("stronghold of the tongue") to minister to someone hurting due to a situation in their own life. (Be-er) God is able to empower you through His grace to encourage others even when you don't feel like it. And since you reap what you sow you end up encouraged yourself.

*Be-er "well"*

We all have strengths and weaknesses. We may spend the majority of our time and energy in one level or another, but the Father's desire is that we come up higher in our weak areas. He wants us to be well balanced in our walk. Therefore we need not be discouraged when we find ourselves back at square one from time to time. Paul describes the newborn Christian as one whose diet consists of milk exclusively. But that doesn't mean that a mature believer never needs milk again. I still enjoy a good glass of milk whenever I eat.

There are as many combinations of valleys and plateaus and the order we negotiate them as there are believers. You will have a predominate level or plateau where you spend the majority of your spiritual existence, all the while visiting and revisiting other places. The various levels are all interrelated and therefore it is necessary to continue to grow in each. Ultimately we want to spend the majority of our time in Pisgah. We may get a glimpse occasionally, but we cannot remain there as long as we have "stuff" in our lives that needs to be purged. Notice I said "stuff." That's not meant as a nice way to say sin. There are things that hinder our relationship with the Father that aren't necessarily sin. Consider this verse from Hebrews 12:1 *"...Let us lay aside every **weight**, and the sin which doth so easily beset us..."* Anything that hinders our relationship with the Father can be considered a weight; hobbies, TV, wrong relationships, and so forth.

To illustrate my point, let's take a little test. For this test there are no right or wrong answers. Just be honest if you want an accurate assessment of where you are spiritually. If you answer objectively I think you will discover you have strengths and weaknesses like the rest of us. Allow me to do a little teaching first so you understand the nature of the test.

In Oboth we discussed the foundation blocks. Once you have a foundation you must proceed to build upon it. 2Peter chapter one instructs us to add to our foundation. Let's begin with verse one, *"Simon Peter, a servant and an apostle of Jesus Christ, to them that have obtained like precious faith with us through the righteousness of God and our Saviour Jesus Christ:"* Notice whom Peter is talking to; "to them who have obtained like precious faith." He is referring to Christians.

Now look at verses five through seven, *"And beside this, giving all diligence, add to your faith virtue; and to virtue knowledge; And to knowledge temperance; and to temperance patience; and to patience godliness; And to godliness brotherly kindness; and to brotherly kindness charity."* We mentioned Oboth is the starting point for every believer. We are saved by grace through faith. Oboth means "mumbling of the Father's name." We were babies but God doesn't want us to stay that way. His desire is for us to grow so that we are better equipped to help others. (Be-er) Okay we have faith, we've laid our foundation, and we want to build on that.

Before we move on there is one more point of interest I'd like to mention. There are seven characteristics we are adding to our faith. Likewise there are seven levels of growth from our starting point at Oboth. God likes the number seven; it represents perfection, maturity, or completion. Hence Oboth and faith are starting points for something, not the final destination. It is not God's plan to save us then allow us to sit and wait for the return of His Son. I'll say more about the correlation between the seven characteristics of growth and the seven levels of maturity at the conclusion of the test. Also keep in mind this is merely an indicator, not "thus saith the Lord." So don't get discouraged. When I initially administered this test to some of the most mature believers I know, there were no perfect scores. (Not even close) Let's briefly examine each of the seven building blocks we are adding to our foundation. This will help you to score yourself during the test.

# SPIRITUAL MATURITY TEST
(Based on 2 Peter 1)

Virtue:  Greek = Arete ("excellence")

Virtue is doing what you know to do is right. My word for it is integrity. It's demonstrating the character of God even when the pressure is on and no one is looking. Striving for excellence in all you do brings glory to the Father.

Knowledge:  Greek = Gnosis ("knowing, aware, understanding")

Knowledge, as it pertains to our test, is best defined by verse three of our text. "According to His divine power hath He given unto us all things pertaining to life and godliness **through the knowledge of Him."** In essence, how well do you know Him and His Word and how well do you apply what you know?

Temperance:  Greek = Egkrateia ("self-control, mastery")

To be temperate is to practice self-control when your flesh is screaming to have its way. That includes emotions, appetites, and pleasures.

**Patience:** Greek = Hupomeno ("to remain under a load or trial, persevere)

We think of patience as the ability to wait. Though that can be a test for us all from time to time, patience as defined here is enduring a more substantial trial. For instance in Hebrews 12:2 when Jesus "endured the cross," the word endured is the same Greek word as Peter used for patience. It's doubtful that any of us will ever be subjected to anything remotely close to what Jesus endured, but I mention this to give you some perspective.

**Godliness:** Greek = Eusebeia ("piety, devout, reverent")

Most people have a tendency to think of godliness as "God like." The Greek word for God is "Theos" which indicates Deity. However our word does describe someone who practices God like principles. In Acts, chapter ten, Luke describes Cornelius as "devout." Why? If you read the entire chapter you will find Cornelius fasted, prayed, and tithed. So godliness, for our test purposes, is how regularly you exercise these principles as led by the Holy Spirit.

*Nahaliel The Valley of God*

**Brotherly:** Greek = Philadelphia ("brotherly love, fraternal affection")

Kindness:

If you recognize the Greek word here as a city in Pennsylvania you are correct. Philadelphia calls itself "the city of brotherly love" Brotherly love is more than patting someone on the back at church and saying I love you. It is dying to ourselves and laying our life down for the brethren. The criteria here is how consistent are you at giving up something you would rather be doing to help a fellow Christian when they need it?

**Charity:** Greek = Agape ("love, affection, benevolence")

This type of love is a step above brotherly love. It has been described as God's kind of love As 1 Corinthians 13 describes it, "love is long suffering, kind, not envious, nor vain, or thin skinned. It doesn't misbehave, isn't selfish, not easily provoked, thinks positive, rejoices in the truth, forbears, believes, hopes, and endures. Wow! How often do we walk in that kind of love? No ulterior motives, no hidden agendas, expecting nothing in return. Only a person with a very close relationship to the Father can walk in this type of relationship on a consistent basis.

*Be-er "well"*

Now that you have an idea what Peter meant when he said, "add to your faith," let's take the test. You already have faith so we all start with one point. If your answer is *never* give yourself a "0". There are seven characteristic traits worth a maximum of seven points each, so 50 would be a perfect score. By the way, if you score 50 you are excused from reading any further; it's difficult to improve upon perfection.

### 1. Virtue
How consistent would you say you walk in integrity?

| 1 | 2 | 3 | 4 | 5 | 6 | 7 |
|---|---|---|---|---|---|---|
| Rarely | Seldom | Occasionally | Often | Usually | Typically | Always |

### 2. Knowledge
Using the words below, how would you describe your ability to know what to do, and do it, when trials come? (Based upon scriptural principles)

| 1 | 2 | 3 | 4 | 5 | 6 | 7 |
|---|---|---|---|---|---|---|
| Rarely | Seldom | Occasionally | Often | Usually | Typically | Always |

### 3. Temperance
How often are you able to practice self-control while your flesh is screaming to do otherwise?

| 1 | 2 | 3 | 4 | 5 | 6 | 7 |
|---|---|---|---|---|---|---|
| Rarely | Seldom | Occasionally | Often | Usually | Typically | Always |

### 4. Patience
While going through trials, how well do you endure without murmuring and complaining?

| 1 | 2 | 3 | 4 | 5 | 6 | 7 |
|---|---|---|---|---|---|---|
| Rarely | Seldom | Occasionally | Often | Usually | Typically | Always |

### 5. Godliness
How often are you obedient when God calls you to fast, pray, and/or give? (Note: fasting, praying, and giving here denotes as specifically instructed by God. Praying and tithing on a regular basis are a given and should not be factored into your choice.)

| 1 | 2 | 3 | 4 | 5 | 6 | 7 |
|---|---|---|---|---|---|---|
| Rarely | Seldom | Occasionally | Often | Usually | Typically | Always |

### 6. Brotherly Kindness
How often when you are impressed to fulfill a need do you sacrifice your own itinerary to help a fellow Christian?

| 1 | 2 | 3 | 4 | 5 | 6 | 7 |
|---|---|---|---|---|---|---|
| Rarely | Seldom | Occasionally | Often | Usually | Typically | Always |

### 7. Charity
How often do you walk in agape love? (Remember: unconditional, with a pure motive, God like love.)

| 1 | 2 | 3 | 4 | 5 | 6 | 7 |
|---|---|---|---|---|---|---|
| Rarely | Seldom | Occasionally | Often | Usually | Typically | Always |

Now you can see what I mean about different levels of maturity in different areas of your life. Don't be discouraged, it's normal. Ask God to help you in your weaker areas. Paul said "when we are weak He is strong." God is more concerned about our growth than we are. All we have to do is cooperate with the Holy Spirit as we are led and we will be on our way to maturity.

I promised I'd say more about the correlation between the seven levels of maturity and the seven characteristics listed in 2 Peter. We all start at Oboth with faith. Our destination is Pisgah where the manifest presence of God resides. God is everywhere, but He is not manifested everywhere. We should desire to be in His presence as often as possible. So what is the correlation? *"God is love."* (1 Jn 4:16) Agape love is our calling, Pisgah is our calling. They coincide, you cannot separate the two. You can't walk in perfect love within your own strength; neither can you enter Pisgah without agape love. In the end it is all about His grace and mercy. He will have mercy upon whomever He wills, but it is our responsibility to maintain our eligibility. And it is His grace, (the divine influence upon the heart and it's reflection in the life) that enables us to pursue Him to greater depths. Jesus demonstrated the character of the Father, so must we.

Jesus knew who He was at twelve, but it was 18 years before He began His ministry. Hebrews 5:8 *says "Though He were a son, yet learned He obedience by the things which He suffered."* If Jesus went through process before being used of the Father it stands to reason we will as well. When our relationship with the Father is one of love, where there are no ulterior motives, just a pure, compassionate heart, then He can trust us to do the works of Jesus. *"Verily, verily I say unto you, he that believeth on me, the works that I do shall he do also; and greater works than these shall he do; because I go unto my Father."* (Jn 14:12)

Why is it so important that we do the works of Jesus; in a word, evangelism. Can you imagine opening the eyes of a blind man, or causing a lame man to walk again? That is demonstrating the Kingdom of God. That is evangelism. After demonstration, proclamation is not an issue. People are hungry for the supernatural. When they cannot find it in the church they look elsewhere. Healing, prophecy, deliverance, etc., are simply tools for evangelism.

The attitude of the heart is the key. We have to mature into agape love to enter Pisgah. Seeing miracles just for the 'wow' factor isn't acceptable. There will be no place for pride. Your desires must line up with His. You cannot fool God, He knows your heart. To be used, like Jesus, you must be in a position of sincere humility; where all the honor and glory goes to the Father. Amen!

I dangled that carrot before you with the hope that your motivation to move forward remains strong. Before we move into the first valley of this phase let me tie 2Peter 1:5-7 together for you. We start with faith once we're born again. We begin to do the things we know are right and in the most excellent manner we are capable of. (**Virtue**) At the same time we seek God through His Word for more **knowledge**. We haven't matured to the point where we walk in the Spirit on a consistent basis, so we practice self-control. (**Temperance**) As we mature through process, (valleys) we learn to endure them better. (**Patience**) Our relationship develops to the point where we seek God through special times of prayer, fasting, and giving. (**Godliness**) The closer we get to the Father the easier it is to realize how far short we come in relation to His character. Yet we discover more and more just how much He loves us in spite of ourselves, so it

*Be-er "well"*

becomes easier to love our brethren. (**Brotherly kindness**) As our compassion and genuine love for others grows so grows our love for our Creator. (**Charity**) BOOM! Open door, the veil is rent in twain, and we enter into the Holy of Holies, Pisgah, the manifest presence of God. Hallelujah! Please understand, this is a process, not a formula.

I hope you caught the correlation between the seven levels of maturity (Oboth to Pisgah) and the seven characteristics of maturity from 2 Peter 1:5-7. Both are progressive in their difficulty to master, yet in either you may be working on more than one level at a time. Regardless of where you are, you can still be a "well" to others. We simply need to listen and obey the Holy Spirit as we are prompted to give of our time and, or, resources. Sowing into others' lives is what Be-er is all about. Reaping what you sow is a Biblical principle found from Genesis to maps. If you are willing to help others in their time of need, then help will be available when you need it.

I want to reiterate that the test was for illustrative purposes. Do not allow the enemy to discourage you or bring condemnation. Are you ready to walk into another valley? If your desire is to grow as a Christian then I bet you are. Let's go!

*Nahaliel The Valley of God*

## Valley of Ajalon ("Strength of a deer")

Let's begin with some background information in order to understand the context of our key verses. Joshua has led Israel in several victorious battles at this point. The Gibeonites, who are nearby, fear for their lives and devise a plan to trick Joshua into forming a league with them. Joshua fails to consult with God and makes what we might call a peace treaty with them. This infuriates the kings of the other nearby cities thus five kings form an alliance to war against the Gibeonites.

Joshua remains true to his word and responds to the Gibeonites plea for help in spite of their deception. Joshua was a loyal ally, a man of integrity. Two characteristics I value in my own relationships. Evidently God does as well because He chose to stand behind Joshua's decision. Remember God didn't initiate this pact between Israel and Gibeon, yet according to our text He comes on board.

*"And the LORD said unto Joshua, Fear them not: for I have delivered them into thine hand; there shall not a man of them stand before thee. Joshua therefore came unto them suddenly, and went up from Gilgal all night. And the LORD*

*discomfited them before Israel, and slew them with a great slaughter at Gibeon, and chased them along the way that goeth up to Bethhoron, and smote them to Azekah, and unto Makkedah. And it came to pass, as they fled from before Israel, and were in the going down to Bethhoron, that the LORD cast down great stones from heaven upon them unto Azekah, and they died: they were more which died with hailstones than they whom the children of Israel slew with the sword. Then spake Joshua to the LORD in the day when the LORD delivered up the Amorites before the children of Israel, and he said in the sight of Israel, Sun, stand thou still upon Gibeon; and thou, Moon, in the valley of Ajalon. And the sun stood still, and the moon stayed, until the people had avenged themselves upon their enemies. Is not this written in the book of Jasher? So the sun stood still in the midst of heaven, and hasted not to go down about a whole day. And there was no day like that before it or after it, that the LORD hearkened unto the voice of a man: for the LORD fought for Israel."* (Josh 10:8-14)

God not only promised Joshua victory, He provided it. He supernaturally destroyed more of the enemy than Israel did in the natural. This shouldn't be surprising, it wasn't the first or the last time that God intervened on behalf of Israel. Divine intervention played a key role throughout the history of Israel. If you take an honest inventory you will find the same is true of your own life. God is no respecter of persons. How often have you taken the first step of faith then God stepped in and did *"exceedingly above all that you asked or thought."*

God's promise to Joshua in chapter one was *"Have not I commanded thee? Be strong and of a good courage; be not afraid, neither be thou dismayed: for the LORD thy God is with thee whithersoever thou goest."* God performed His promise for Joshua and He will do the same for you. The

Word says *"the battle belongs to the Lord"* and *"it's not by (our) might, nor by (our) power, but by My Spirit saith the Lord"*

If you are to conquer Ajalon and desire the strength of a deer, then you must begin with a strong relationship with the Father. As David wrote in Psalm 42 *"As the deer panteth after the Waterbrook, so panteth my soul after thee O God."* A deer will risk everything, including its life to get to water when thirsty. Are you that determined to have a relationship with the Father? Are you willing to sacrifice your time, your reputation, or perhaps even your life to develop your relationship with God? When I say life I don't necessarily mean literally; God doesn't need martyrs. He wants people to *live* for Him; the only dying necessary is of our flesh. Enoch loved God and was translated. Elijah knew God and was caught up to Heaven in a chariot. Moses changed the mind of God, David was a man after God's own heart, and Joshua influenced God to make time stand still.

How will God show Himself strong in your life? What feats will you accomplish through His power? Your desire for Him, His heart (not His hand), will be the determining factor in the degree to which you are used of Him. I have often heard prominent men and women of God use the phrase "we are seeking His hand and not His face." Basically what they mean is we tend to desire the *things* God can give us instead of desiring a *relationship* with Him. Recently God spoke to me with an amendment to that phrase. He said, "People are seeking My mind and not My face." In other words we have moved our emphasis from *thing*s to knowledge. There is nothing wrong with seeking the mind of Christ. In fact that is scriptural. The problem lies with our motives. If you're seeking knowledge for the sake of knowledge and not relationship, you are still missing the mark. It's nothing more than pride. Paul confronted those who used this practice at Mars

*Be-er "well"*

Hill in Acts 17:21, 22. *"For all the Athenians and strangers which were there spent their time in nothing else, but to tell, or to hear some new thing. Then Paul stood in the midst of Mars Hill, and said, Ye men of Athens, I perceive that in all things ye are too <u>superstitious."</u>* (Religious)

It is wise to stay attuned to our motives. The supernatural always supersedes the natural. The prefix "super" means above and beyond. We are capable of doing bigger and better things when we allow God to work through us as opposed to "figuring things out" on our own. God will do exploits above and beyond anything we can ask or think when our relationship is as the deer panting for the water brook. Our motive must be to experience Him, not what He can tell us or what He can do for us.

*"And it came to pass, when they brought out those kings unto Joshua, that Joshua called for all the men of Israel, and said unto the captains of the men of war which went with him, Come near, put your feet upon the necks of these kings. And they came near, and put their feet upon the necks of them. And Joshua said unto them, Fear not, nor be dismayed, be strong and of good courage: for thus shall the LORD do to all your enemies against whom ye fight."* (Josh 10:24, 25)

At Be-er we become a well of life to others. We have tasted the water, experienced it, and now we must share it. Joshua shares the promise God gave him with the warriors of Israel. Notice what he commands the captains to do in verse 24, *"put your feet upon the necks of these kings."* Joshua wanted to demonstrate that as long as their hearts were after God, the enemy would be under their feet. This principle is demonstrated from Genesis 3 to Revelation 20. The authority of the believer is just one example of the benefits included in the atonement that we should be sharing as part of the gospel.

The authority of the believer is another topic that has been discussed immensely among the body of Christ. There are plenty of materials available on the subject, and it merits more study than I propose to submit at this time. However, I do feel inclined to offer you a few thoughts to ponder.

1) In my introduction I explained why Moses lifted up the serpent of brass; to demonstrate God's authority over the enemy.
2) Adam relinquished his authority in the garden.
3) Jesus restored authority to man by way of the cross.
4) *"Verily, verily, I say unto you, He that believeth on me, the works that I do shall he do also; and greater works than these shall he do; because I go unto my Father."* (Jn 14:12)

Be-er is a place of ministering. Jesus said He came not to be ministered to, but to minister. Serving others utilizing our spiritual gifts is just one avenue of ministering the Gospel to the lost. Understanding the authority God has entrusted us with is imperative to operating in the Spirit to our fullest potential, and making the greatest impact for the Kingdom of God.

*Be-er "well"*

## **Valley of Jezreel** (God will sow)

This valley differs from our previous valleys in several ways. Most of the valleys are referred to in more than one passage, but by the same name. Jezreel is an exception. It is the name of two cities, a valley, and three individuals. It is also referred to by two different names at times to emphasize the point being made in that particular passage. We will discuss the valley of Jezreel as it is recorded in the book of Judges. For further demonstration of the principles we are studying, you may wish to examine the book of Revelation where it is referred to as Armageddon.

In both scenarios the circumstances and the outcome are similar. The situation seems hopeless, the odds are overwhelming. But God loves a handicap. What is impossible for man is a walk in the park for God. It gives Him an opportunity to demonstrate His power. Mankind is just along for the ride. Both passages make it obvious you do not want to be on the receiving end of God's wrath. You can read of Armageddon in Revelation chapter 16. To illustrate our point we will focus on Jezreel as portrayed in the book of Judges.

Let's begin with our first passage from Judges 6:33. *"Then all the Midianites and the Amalekites and the children of the east were gathered together, and went over, and pitched in the valley of Jezreel."* If you read the entire chapter you will find that the enemy was referred in number as *"grasshoppers for multitude; for both they and their camels were without number: and they entered into the land to destroy it."* Jesus tells us in John 10:10 that *"The enemy comes to kill, steal, and destroy."* In case you didn't know it, the devil hates you. He wants to kill your dreams and visions, steal your hope and joy, and destroy your land. (Think of land as your heart for God.)

Israel brought this attack on themselves. They had *"did evil in the sight of the Lord"* (vs.51), by setting up an altar to baal and constructing groves (images of idols). God operates on principles, one of which can be stated as:

### Obedience = Hedge Up
### Disobedience = Hedge Down

A hedge represents God's protection. Do you remember in the book of Job where God was telling satan about Job, *"And the LORD said unto satan, Hast thou considered my servant Job, that there is none like him in the earth, a perfect and an upright man, one that feareth God, and escheweth evil?"* Notice what the devil replied, *"Hast not thou made an **hedge** about him, and about his house, and about all that he hath on every side? thou hast blessed the work of his hands, and his substance is increased in the land."* A literal hedge doesn't hinder an evil spirit, but an angel can.

*Be-er "well"*

I don't presume to be an expert on the fascinating subject of Angels, howbeit, I would like to share something here. Revelation 9:16 refers to 200 million demons reserved just for one short period of the great tribulation. If that's just a portion of the total number of demons, and there are twice as many angels as demons, how many angels are there? Obviously, there are enough angels to provide a hedge for us all as long as we are obedient.

So do bad things happen only when we're disobedient? No. It rains on the just and the unjust. (Matt 5:45) Job, according to the Word of God, was *"a perfect and an upright man, one that feareth God, and escheweth evil."* Job wasn't disobedient, so why was he forced to endure such an attack? Job 3:25 does indicate a possible opening for the enemy; *"For the thing which I greatly feared is come upon me, and that which I was afraid of is come unto me."* Fear is the opposite of faith and provides an inroad for a demonic attack.

Disobedience is a sin, whether by commission or omission, and it gives the enemy an opportunity to intrude in your life. Israel had committed the sin of idolatry and chose to cry out to God only after becoming impoverished and helpless against a formidable enemy. The Lord sent them a prophet to inform them that He had delivered them from Egypt, gave them the land, and dominion, *"but ye have not obeyed my voice."* (Judges 6:10)

It doesn't appear Israel repented because there is no mention of any action on their part to reconcile with God. They didn't remove the groves or destroy their idols. Yet God demonstrated His mercy by appointing a deliverer, Gideon. God inspired Gideon to cut down the groves, destroy the altar of baal, and build an altar to the Lord. By the way Gideon's name means "to hew down, destroy."

In chapter 7 God does something very interesting. He arranges the odds on the enemies favor 450:1. When I said earlier God likes a handicap, I wasn't exaggerating. By reducing Gideon's army from 32,000 to 300 God positioned Himself to make an impressive statement. *"It's not by might, nor by power, but by My Spirit saith the Lord." "And the LORD said unto Gideon, The people that are with thee are too many for me to give the Midianites into their hands, lest Israel vaunt themselves against me, saying, Mine own hand hath saved me. Now therefore go to, proclaim in the ears of the people, saying, Whosoever is fearful and afraid, let him return and depart early from mount Gilead. And there returned of the people twenty and two thousand; and there remained ten thousand. And the LORD said unto Gideon, The people are yet too many; bring them down unto the water, and I will try them for thee there: and it shall be, that of whom I say unto thee, This shall go with thee, the same shall go with thee; and of whomsoever I say unto thee, This shall not go with thee, the same shall not go. So he brought down the people unto the water: and the LORD said unto Gideon, Every one that lappeth of the water with his tongue, as a dog lappeth, him shalt thou set by himself; likewise every one that boweth down upon his knees to drink. And the number of them that lapped, putting their hand to their mouth, were three hundred men: but all the rest of the people bowed down upon their knees to drink water. And the LORD said unto Gideon, By the three hundred men that lapped will I save you, and deliver the Midianites into thine hand: and let all the other people go every man unto his place."* (Judges 7:2-7)

A key element to this story is the Glory of God and the humility of Gideon. Paul wrote in 1Corinthians 1:29 *"That no flesh should glory in his presence."* The word *glory* here means "to boast." We have nothing to boast about. Our next breath is a gift from God. Any gift, talent, or wisdom we have is by the grace of God. Paul went on to say in verse 31, *"he that glorieth, (boasts) let him glory (boast) in the Lord."* Anything we do that is worthwhile is of God; it's Christ, (the anointed one and His anointing) that manifests through us. If we ever get a revelation of that we will have a lot less pride in our lives. Finally, in this regard, consider what God said through Isaiah in Isaiah 42:8 *"I am the LORD: that is my name: and my glory will I not give to another, neither my praise to graven images."*

Gideon's army is a practical example of God's perspective concerning His might, not ours; His power, not ours. And His Spirit working through those that make themselves available. We need to discover His criteria and strive to realize His standards instead of manufacturing our own. Gideon wasn't chosen for his abilities. He was humble, available, and willing. His army was chosen in like manner.

Let's examine the criteria God used in this particular situation. In verse three the original army was numbered at 32,000. God instructed Gideon to allow the "fainthearted" to return home. Twenty-two thousand chose to depart, leaving 10,000 men to oppose 135,000 enemy soldiers. But God wasn't done yet. He wanted to make the odds even greater against Israel so that He could demonstrate His own power. God administered a test that only 300 of the 10,000 passed. That left 300 men of Israel to face 135,000 "ites." The odds are now 450:1. Israel, like so many of us, is facing a seemingly overwhelming deficit. God has us right where He wants us. There is nowhere to hide, no one to trust, and no place to look but up. He has given us a word just as He did Gideon. Will we believe it? Will we trust Him through it all? Herein lies the key to our spiritual lives, do we believe? When asked *"what shall we do that we might work the works of God,"* Jesus replied *"believe on whom He hath sent."* (Jn 6:28, 29)

To believe or to have faith in something is not just mental assent. James acknowledges the fact that *"the devils also believe and tremble."* The Marines are "looking for a few good men," God is looking for a few men and women of faith. God is seeking men and women who believe to the point that they are radically obedient. Verses 4-7 describe the test that was used to alleviate 9,700 men. God already knew their hearts; He could have chosen His remnant beforehand. Why did He do it this way? I don't have all the answers but I will share some things the Spirit showed me.

First, let's consider the "fearful and afraid" for a moment. Hebrews 11:6 tells us *"But without faith it is impossible to please him: for he that cometh to God must believe that he is, and that he is a rewarder of them that diligently seek him."* You cannot please God while living in fear. Granted, we should have a healthy respect for electricity, heights, poisonous snakes, etc., but not a paralyzing fear.

The fainthearted Christian is akin to the "double minded" man spoken of in James 1:8. *"A double minded man is unstable in all his ways."* Anything unstable is unpredictable; it may or may not perform satisfactorily. Gideon certainly didn't need 22,000 problematic forces like that in this situation. He needed men of faith, he was about to face an army that had a sizeable advantage.

God is still searching the hearts of men and women. He is seeking those who will stand with stability in the face of an enemy who *appears* to be superior; men and women who know *"Greater is He that is in you, than he that is in the world"* (1Jn 4:4). Amen! This isn't something you can "work up" on the spur of the moment. This is a characteristic that must

*Be-er "well"*

be developed through process. When the test comes faith meets it head on and stands for the glory of God.

Ten thousand men of faith remain, about a third of the original army. It's an honor to be among the elite. I served in the US Army with the Rangers during active duty and with Special Forces during my reserve time. Let's call the remaining 10,000 men our Special Forces. But God wasn't done; He wanted the best of the best. To further distinguish yourself, to be the best of the best (in the natural) is more challenging still. It's not for everyone, but God "wires" some of us that way. You must have the mental and physical capacity to endure, but most importantly, the heart. Spiritually speaking it's all about heart.

There is an army God is raising up who not only has the faith, they also have a heart for God. When they say "though none go with me, still I will follow" they mean it. Rangers, Special Forces, Seals, and Delta Force all work in small units. Teams comprised of men with various skills that form a close knit cohesive unit. God has blessed us all with spiritual gifts. He is putting together small contingents of "Special Forces" all around the world to carry out strategic end time tasks. I'm talking about the remnant again.

The valley of Jezreel isn't so much a faith test as it is a heart test. Succeed here and "God will sow" you into His ministry. What is the criterion that qualifies us to be among the elite 300? I've emphasized heart, but also experience through process. The 300 chosen demonstrated their faith, their heart, as well as their experience. Delta Force operatives are selected primarily from among the other elite branches of the Armed Services. To be a candidate you must have at least 50 months of service, the rank of staff sergeant, and no disciplinary problems. Equated to God's elite you could say, "Not a novice, of good report, sober minded, and able to rule well." (Qualifications for a Bishop from 1Timothy 3) Am I implying you have to be a Bishop to be in the remnant of God? No. Bishop means "superintendent" or "overseer." There will be Bishops in the remnant, obviously, but you do not have to hold the office of a bishop to qualify. You will, however, have to be mature, experienced, and living a victorious life in Christ.

Notice what the 300 men did differently than the others. They remained in a position to watch for the enemy while they drank. All 10,000 drank of the water but their posture in doing so differed. Watching implies relationship and obedience. When you are positioned correctly with the Father you will hear His instructions. You will see what He's up to and be in position to see the enemy approaching. You will also be less likely to be attacked when the enemy knows you are prepared.

The devil is cowardly, he wants to blindside you. He doesn't fight fair, he would rather hit you when you aren't looking, then kick you while you're down. The Bible is clear; "Watch and pray," "watch and be sober," "watch and stand fast," and "watch with thanksgiving." (Mt 26:41/ 1Th 5:6/ 1Cor 16:13/ Col 4:2) My favorite is Luke 12:37, *"Blessed are those servants, whom the lord when he cometh shall find watching: verily I say unto you, that he shall gird himself, and make them to sit down to meat, and will come forth and serve them."* There is much to be said about watching. My prayer is that you and I will be like Jesus, who watched His Father continuously and did only what He saw the Father do.

Now look at verse 15, *"And it was so, when Gideon heard the telling of the dream, and the interpretation thereof, that he worshipped, and returned into the host of Israel, and said, Arise; for the LORD hath delivered into your hand the host of Midian."* I believe this was a turning point for Gideon.

*Be-er "well"*

Through process his faith had grown, he had graduated to a PHD level. (Past Having Doubt) He worshipped the Lord. We generally wait until after the fact before we worship the Lord. Learn to worship God when He sows, not just when the harvest comes. This is a true sign of maturity and a definite plus when travelling through Jezreel.

Once you know that you know that you have heard from the Lord, it's time to act. Let's finish the valley of Jezreel with the account of Gideon's victory. *"So Gideon, and the hundred men that were with him, came unto the outside of the camp in the beginning of the middle watch; and they had but newly set the watch: and they blew the trumpets, and brake the pitchers that were in their hands. And the three companies blew the trumpets, and brake the pitchers, and held the lamps in their left hands, and the trumpets in their right hands to blow withal: and they cried, The sword of the LORD, and of Gideon. And they stood every man in his place round about the camp; and all the host ran, and cried, and fled. And the three hundred blew the trumpets, and the LORD set every man's sword against his fellow, even throughout all the host: and the host fled to Bethshittah in Zererath, and to the border of Abelmeholah, unto Tabbath."*

From the outset we find Gideon had a divinely inspired battle plan. From verse 19 we see that the timing was important. The middle watch represents the 10pm – 2am shift. Verse 19 states the attack began at the beginning of the watch. This is an excellent strategy because the guards are most likely distracted and tired. They are probably more concerned about being relieved than they are about their duties. A timely attack creates confusion and can quickly escalate into chaos.

Imagine yourself in a quiet room, it's dark, peaceful, you are very relaxed and confident. Suddenly the door flies open, you hear the blast of a trumpet, glass is breaking, and there are bright lights in your eyes. You're temporarily blinded, confused, startled, and most likely scared. Pandemonium ensues. What's happening? Then it registers, *"and they cried, The sword of the LORD, and of Gideon."* You find your sword and begin swinging at the first available target. In survival mode, fueled by fear, you inadvertently turn on your own comrades. This was the fate of the Midianites.

1Corinthians 1:27 says *"But God hath chosen the foolish things of the world to confound the wise; and God hath chosen the weak things of the world to confound the things which are mighty."* Why? Verse 29 goes on to say *"That no flesh should glory in his presence."* God demonstrates His ability to use a small remnant to overcome the enemy throughout the Word. The greater the odds were against Him, the greater the glory.

What can we ascertain spiritually from the account of Gideon's strategy?

**Process–empty vessel:**
empty of ourselves/broken = fit for the Masters use

**Demonstration–lamp:**
light within/ Spirit led life showing forth His glory

**Proclamation–trumpet:**
a sound/voice = announcement/message

Do not "blow an uncertain sound." *"For if the trumpet give an uncertain sound, who shall prepare himself to the battle?"* (1Corinthians 14:8) Let your voice proclaim the truth of the gospel. The truth is easier to communicate when you have experienced it. By submitting yourself to process, and coming out victorious, you are in a much better position to witness. Empty yourself of the flesh through process. *"The sacrifices of God are a broken spirit: a broken and a contrite heart, O*

*God, thou wilt not despise."* (Psalms 51:17) Furthermore, if you *"Let your light so shine before men, that they may see your good works, and glorify your Father which is in heaven"* (Matthew 5:16), you will have a captive audience.

It seems to me that, for the most part, the church today is so consumed with the "Great Commission" they forget, *"And these signs shall follow them that believe; In my name shall they cast out devils; they shall speak with new tongues; They shall take up serpents; and if they drink any deadly thing, it shall not hurt them; they shall lay hands on the sick, and they shall recover."* Don't misunderstand me, I do not wish to demean the importance of witnessing to the world. I'm simply stating how much more effective it would be if we were able to demonstrate beforehand. After all isn't that how Jesus did it?

How does a small group such as a family unit, a church, or the remnant overcome superior odds? Imagine how loud 300 trumpets blowing in unison would be. Then add the noise of breaking glass and being blinded by an instantaneous light. The body of Christ needs a **loud** voice, not of one person, but in unison. Its message should be **loud**, *"Repent: for the Kingdom of Heaven is at hand."* (Matthew 4:17) Our vessels should be broken. He is the potter, we are the clay. We must allow Him to fashion us after His will. Our lights should be bright, bringing the darkness to naught; demonstrating the Kingdom of God through the power of the Spirit. I emphasize the word **loud** here because that is how the apostles turned the world upside down. We, as the body of Christ need to be **LOUD!** I utilized the "**LOUD**" acronym back in Oboth, but I feel it"s necessary to repeat.

**Love**: The foundation of God's Kingdom is love. We must love Him first and others second. Without love we cannot win the world to Christ.

**Order**: God is a God of order. We must quit conducting church business man's way, through tradition and our own wisdom. God is very specific about the government of His church.

**Unity**: One mind, one accord = power. It's in unity that God commands the blessing. (Psalm 133) Our unity is in our faith in Jesus Christ, not every jot and tittle.

**Discipleship**: Jesus dedicated His ministry discipling others. It is our responsibility to train others as well. It is of mutual benefit; as we pour ourselves into others God pours Himself into us.

The valley of Jezreel is about becoming one of the remnant. God wants to sow into your life so that you will be LOUD for Him. Our responsibility is to prepare the land, (our hearts.) "*Break up your fallow ground: for it is time to seek the LORD, till he come and rain righteousness upon you.*" (Hosea 10:12)

It is possible to watch and work simultaneously as Gideon's 300 did or as Nehemiah instructed his people to do when building the wall. By staying in tune with the Father we are able to see what He is doing and then get in on it. That is faith and works in action. That is what makes a mighty man or woman of valor.

**Chapter 7**

**MATTANAH** "Present or Offering"

# CHAPTER 7
# Mattanah (Present/Offering)

Mattanah is where we present ourselves a living sacrifice to the Lord. We become the offering. We have all said it before "Lord, I lay it all down before you," and at the time we were as serious as we knew how. Mattanah is where we actually do it. We offer our service to God without delay, excuse, or remorse. We become a person who truly walks in the Spirit. Mattanah represents the mature Christian who realizes his or her life is not their own.

Once there was an Indian who desired a relationship with God. He drew a circle in the dirt and placed his tomahawk in it. "Lord I give you my weapon," believing his generosity would win the Lord over. But God replied "I don't want your tomahawk." So the Indian added his spear to the circle and said "Lord I made this myself, it's hand-carved and has beautiful engravings. It's yours." The Lord answered "But I don't want your spear." The Indian started feeling a little anxious but decided to press on, "Lord this is my head dress, it represents my authority and all that I am. I want you to have it." Once again the Lord refused the offering "I don't want your head dress." Finally, exasperated, after giving all he had, the Indian decided to try one more thing. He stepped into the circle and said "Lord, I give you myself." He immediately saw the wisdom of his action when he noticed the smile on

163

God's face. Then he heard the Lord's welcome reply "that's all I ever wanted."

The Indian finally got it, have we? We say "here I am Lord, use me," as long as you don't interfere with my itinerary. We cannot maintain this level of maturity if we continue to entertain our flesh. Jesus is the groom, we are the bride. We are supposed to be married, not dating. Our hobbies, relationships, careers, etc., etc., should never become our primary focus. God tells us to love Him with all our heart, soul, and mind. We're not doing that if we are continuously doing our own thing.

Jesus said *"If you love me, keep My commandments."* (Jn 14:15) Many of us have selective hearing. For instance, we have this overwhelming urge to do something but we dismiss it because it's our bowling night. Or we may feel the Lord leading us to witness or minister to someone but find some rational to excuse ourselves.

I can tell you from experience, you may not get another opportunity. Years ago, I was so busy doing "the Lord's work," that I had little time for God. One of our deacons had cancer and I sensed the Holy Spirit leading me to visit him. Since I had already had a hectic day and the next evening was my normal visitation night, I dismissed the urging of the Spirit. "I'll see him tomorrow I thought." He died before I ever had the opportunity. I don't believe his death was my fault but I do know I was disobedient.

We will not realize the consequences of our delays, selective hearing, disobedience, or selfishness to the full extent in this lifetime. However, one day we will all stand before the judgment seat of Christ to give an account for our actions after we were born again. It isn't wise to casually date Jesus, grieve the Holy Spirit, or disobey the Father.

*Mattanah (present/offering)*

If you want to go to Mattanah you will have to be willing to *"present your bodies a living sacrifice, holy, acceptable unto God, which is your reasonable service."* (Rom 12:1) We don't become perfect at Mattanah, we become willing. We choose the Father over the world. *"And be not conformed to this world: but be ye transformed by the renewing of your mind, that ye may prove what is that good, and acceptable, and perfect, will of God."* (Rom 12:2)

Our aspirations change at Mattanah. We strive to please the Father instead of ourselves or others. We accomplish that through faith. *"But without faith it is impossible to please him: for he that cometh to God must believe that he is, and that he is a rewarder of them that diligently seek him."* (Heb 12:6) By faith we hear Him and by faith we act on what we've heard. We take every opportunity to serve Him. That's our reasonable service. After all, Jesus paid the ultimate price. He *presented* Himself to mankind only to be rejected, and then *offered* Himself as the substitute for our sins. That is Mattanah, "present/ offering." Are you willing to do as the Indian and step into the circle? If so then strive to reach Mattanah and beyond.

We're on our way to Pisgah. There is only one more stop after Mattanah and that is Bamoth. Bamoth means "high elevation," and you have to be in pretty good shape to negotiate the ascent. If you are still motivated to grow as a Christian, the rewards will make the journey worthwhile. There is nothing on earth that compares with the manifest presence of God. Are you willing to challenge the enemy, your flesh, and the world system to move on? Good, then get your hiking boots and let's get started.

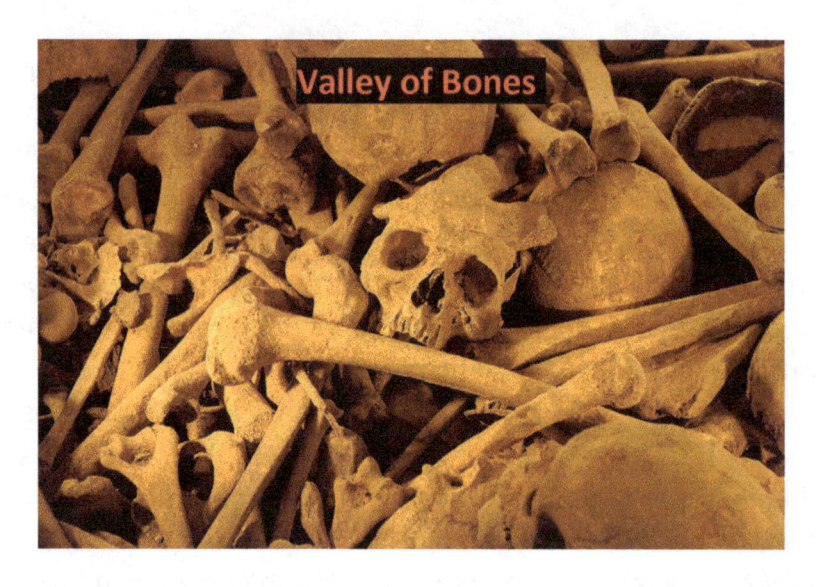

## Valley of Bones

This is a unique valley in that it is not an actual place. It represents a spiritual condition. Ezekiel 36 contains a prophecy of the Holy Spirit indwelling the New Testament body. In chapter 38 Ezekiel warns us of Armageddon, the site of the last battle man will ever be involved in. It seems very probable that the chapter between these two events, chapter 37, contains prophecy concerning the early church period unto the present. We are the latter day church, ergo this vision is relevant to us. Let's examine what Ezekiel saw.

I'm not a pessimistic person but I am realistic; for the most part the church is *dry*. Dry in the Hebrew means "ashamed, confused, disappointed; to dry up and or wither." God is still moving, He's performing miracles every day. And there are churches that are thriving, filled with the Spirit, and prospering. But for the most part the body of Christ is lacking. We have went our own way, created our own "dry" doctrine, substituted programs for presence and a feel good theology

## Mattanah (present/offering)

for anointing. There is nothing wrong with doctrine, programs, or theology. The problem lies with their origin. When devised out of man's wisdom they dry up, wither, cause shame, confusion and disappointment.

What do I mean by "feel good theology?" Have you ever been to a service where "the spirit was so thick you could cut it with a knife?" Goose bumps were the order of the day. People raising their hands, shouting, dancing, perhaps even some aisle running. The preaching was "off the hook" as they say in today's vernacular. Then reality sets in. You leave the building and argue with your spouse all the way to the car about his or her behavior. You really can't remember anything practical the preacher said. You're not sure why it all seemed so exciting, but you felt good, at the time.

There is nothing wrong with emotions in a church service. God gave us emotions and I enjoy expressing mine when God is moving in a service. But is God moving? Is anyone repenting, getting saved, delivered, healed, or is reconciliation taking place? Was it an emotionally inspired service or a Spirit led service? I'm not implying that if nothing dramatic takes place God wasn't in it. What I am saying is that it is difficult to place the Spirit of God on a time limit, (preferably between 11:00 and 12:00) then dictate to Him the type of service we prefer that day. Getting "charged up" emotionally isn't going to get us through the day, much less through the week and beyond. We need edification, not pacification.

Consider these two passages of scripture that speak of the latter day church, beginning with 2Timothy 3:1-4. *"This know also, that in the last days perilous times shall come For men shall be lovers of their own selves, covetous, boasters, proud, blasphemers, disobedient to parents, unthankful, unholy, Without natural affection, trucebreakers, false accusers, incontinent, fierce, despisers of those that are good,*

*Traitors, heady, highminded, lovers of pleasures more than lovers of God."* And Revelation 3:14-17 *"And unto the angel of the church of the Laodiceans write; These things saith the Amen, the faithful and true witness, the beginning of the creation of God; I know thy works, that thou art neither cold nor hot: I would thou wert cold or hot. So then because thou art lukewarm, and neither cold nor hot, I will spue thee out of my mouth. Because thou sayest, I am rich, and increased with goods, and have need of nothing; and knowest not that thou art wretched, and miserable, and poor, and blind, and naked."* Does this sound like us?

Twice I have discussed the concept of being LOUD. The "D" in loud was discipleship. The Valley of Bones illustrates our need for discipleship, the concept of mentoring pupils. Churches differ in mission and purpose; however they should all have a strong propensity towards edification and spiritual growth. Edify means to build up or mature. If we truly presented ourselves as an offering at Mattanah we will be seeking to edify the body of Christ.

I'm going to venture off on what may seem to be a rabbit trail to you but I assure you this is pertinent. There are two basic types of Spiritual gifting. The Doma gifts: apostles, prophets, evangelists, pastors, and teachers. (Eph 4:11) Then there are the charismatic gifts listed as listed in 1Corinthians 12:8-10, (not all inclusive). Both are to "perfect the body" (1Cor 12:7) unto edification (1Cor 14:26). *"For the perfecting of the saints, for the work of the ministry, for the edifying of the body of Christ: Till we all come in the unity of the faith, and of the knowledge of the Son of God, unto a perfect man, unto the measure of the stature of the fulness of Christ."* (Eph 4:12, 13) Stay with me, we're going somewhere.

Edifying the body to maturity until it reaches the *full measure of Christ* is what this valley is all about. Nothing can build

*Mattanah (present/offering)*

your faith and make a more lasting impression than being in the manifest presence of God. The emotions that accompany His presence are genuine and effect positive change within you. Whereas hype, whipped to a frenzy, tickle my ears, entertaining theology causes emotion that is short term and produces little or no change.

I've stated more than once that we all go through the valleys more than once, to various degrees, and at different times than others. To obtain victory in this valley you must successfully traverse several others first. The Valley of bones requires the use of the combined skills acquired through the process incurred during the previous levels. For example, the thoughts, speech, vision, strength, and faith you developed along the way become essential tools to accomplish the mandate set forth in this valley.

Moving forward in our key text will help you understand what I'm getting at. *"And he said unto me, Son of man, can these bones live? And I answered, O Lord GOD, thou knowest."* Ezekiel was written over 2500 years ago and this question is still pertinent today. The bones are scattered everywhere. They are dry, without life. Can the body of Christ unite? Can we live as God intended? According to the Word of God we are not only able, we will.

Jesus is coming back for a glorious church, one without spot or wrinkle, a united body. *"That he might present it to himself a glorious church, not having spot, or wrinkle, or any such thing; but that it should be holy and without blemish."* (Eph 5:27) Look at Ephesians 4:13 again, *"Till we all come in the unity of the faith."* The interpretation of the word "till" here is unique to this passage. It is the only time this form of the word was used in the Bible. It doesn't mean *if* nor does it pertain to time. The rendering here is "as far as." Paul is speaking of the purpose for the fivefold ministry in this chapter. He is saying that the church government will edify the body of Christ "as far as" *"the unity of the faith"* can take us, which would be *"unto the measure of the stature of the fulness of Christ."* Herein lies the "O" and the "U" in our acronym LOUD. Order and unity are essential traits to the success of the end time church when it comes to evangelism and discipleship.

Unity is not an option. The valley of Bones is a spiritual depiction of what Jesus spoke of often, unity. John 17:21 is a prime example, *"That they all may be one; as thou, Father, art in me, and I in thee, that they also may be one in us: that the world may believe that thou hast sent me."* Unity is vital to evangelism. Jesus reiterates in the following two verses *"And the glory which thou gavest me I have given them; that they may be one, even as we are one: I in them, and thou in me, that they may be made perfect in one; and **that the world may know** that thou hast sent me, and hast loved them, as thou hast loved me."* (emphasis mine) If there is any doubt as to whom He is speaking consider verse 20 *"Neither pray I for these alone, but for them also which shall believe on me through their word."*

What is our part in this valley? Can these bones live? *"Again he said unto me, Prophesy upon these bones, and say unto them, O ye dry bones, hear the word of the LORD."* We must start prophesying to the body, beginning with our own. In chapter 3 I stated you are the prophet of your own life. In your words are life and death. (Prov 18:21) Hopefully you have been practicing speaking the Word over your own life. In this valley you will discover the importance of speaking the Word over the body of Christ.

The first key is found in verse one of our text. *"The hand of the LORD was upon me, and carried me out in the spirit of the LORD, and set me down in the midst of the valley which was full of bones."* (Ezek 37:1) We must rely upon the wisdom and leadership of the Lord. *"Trust in the LORD with all thine heart; and lean not unto thine own understanding. In all thy ways acknowledge him, and he shall direct thy paths."* (Prov 3:5, 6) When we choose to go our own way and trust in our own wisdom, we are setting ourselves up for failure. As we mature from level to level we become better equipped to hear and obey the Spirit.

There is a price to pay for every level of anointing and maturity. It's what we've been calling process. It's in the valleys that we learn what we're made of. Were you made to trust the Lord? Yes! Were you made to hear His Word and to speak it? Yes! Then trust Him to speak through you concerning His body, the church. He is depending on it. Jesus died for it, He loves it, and in fact depends upon it to advance His Kingdom.

Verse five says *"thus saith the Lord GOD unto these bones; Behold, I will cause breath to enter into you, and ye shall live."* God is the life giver. He longs for His body to live. In the beginning God breathed into man and he became a living soul. (Gen 2:7) Our next breath is in His hand. (Dan 5:23) God is telling us through Ezekiel that He wants new life in the body, not just physical, but spiritual life.

The spiritual life the Father desires for us is not just for us, it has a purpose. The relationship that we develop through spiritual intimacy will enable us to become conduits of His power. As we speak His Word He will breathe new life into His body. God's original intent was to fellowship with man, He fellowshipped with Adam on a daily basis. We, like Adam, have a free will and most of us have opted to ignore our Creator. Many of us who meet in a building with some form of His name on a sign outside are still going our own way. Relationship is not about a building, it's not about a label, it's all about your heart condition. Your heart pumps blood throughout the body but it needs oxygen. Are you getting any oxygen? Are you breathing, or are you dry?

(Ezek 37:6) **God will:**  1) Cause us to come together in the unity of the faith.
2) Cover us with His glory as in the beginning
3) Breathe new life into us through the Holy Spirit

God doesn't need our help but He chose to use us anyway. He wants us to prophesy to one another and to the body as a whole. You do not have to hold the office of a Prophet in order to prophesy. Prophecy is simply repeating what you hear the Lord saying. So if you can hear you can prophesy. If you aren't hearing what the Lord is saying in a particular matter don't act until you do. Also keep in mind the Lord will never tell you anything that is contrary to His Word. If you believe you have a Word from the Lord and it seems contradictory to scripture, you either heard wrong or you may have to reconsider some of your theology. Confer with an elder. Another thing to remember is *"the spirits of the prophets are subject to the prophets."* (1Cor 14:32) In other words you don't have to repeat every single thing you hear the moment you hear it. It takes experience to know where and when to say "thus saith the Lord." Timing is of the essence for a word of prophecy to be anointed. The subject matter is beyond the scope of this book, but there are some good resources available if you wish to study prophecy further.

In John 10:10 Jesus said *"I am come that they might have life, and that they might have it more abundantly."* It is Jesus that makes the abundant life possible by His sacrifice at Calvary. He then sent us the Holy Spirit to help us attain and maintain the lifestyle He promised. In order to receive that promise we must establish and maintain relationship with our creator. *"My sheep hear my voice, and I know them, and they follow me."* (Jn 10:27) Hearing His voice and obeying Him is akin to Adam

*Mattanah (present/offering)*

walking with God in the garden during the cool of the day. It is fellowship as God originally designed it to be. It is walking in the Spirit on a consistent basis; that is abundant life.

Before we can experience the Glory of His presence there must be a shaking.

*"So I prophesied as I was commanded: and as I prophesied, there was a noise, and behold a shaking, and the bones came together, bone to his bone."* (Ezek 37:7) In the last chapter we read about Gideon and how he sounded the trumpets, broke the vessels, and exposed the light. We need that noise today to come from our hearts. The sound God desires is one of repentance, in unison, from a remnant of willing vessels. Vessels that have been shook to the breaking point, allowing the light to shine forth.

When the remnant cries out in repentance the shaking will come. Everything that God hasn't ordained will fall. Programs, ministries, improper use of the media, and some ministers will not be able to stand before a Holy God. The dross will be removed and left behind.

Can you picture Elijah in a cave hiding from Jezebel? He thinks he is the only person left serving the Lord. But God said *"Go forth, and stand upon the mount before the LORD. And, behold, the LORD passed by, and a great and strong wind rent the mountains, and brake in pieces the rocks before the LORD; but the LORD was not in the wind: and after the wind an earthquake; but the LORD was not in the earthquake. And after the earthquake a fire; but the LORD was not in the fire: and after the fire a still small voice."* (1Kings 19:11, 12) Simply put, the picture is one of removing the junk so that we can hear. The wind blows away obstacles, the earthquake shakes them, and then the fire purges them. What is left is pure; the dross is removed so that we are in a better position to fellowship with our God.

In verse eight of our key text we see the beginning manifestation of the prophecy given in verse six. *"And when I beheld, lo, the sinews and the flesh came up upon them, and the skin covered them above: but there was no breath in them."* Notice there is still no breath, no life in them. The remnant is like a global puzzle. God is putting the pieces together, after all Jesus said *He* would build His church. We have a glimpse of what the church is supposed to look like but there is still no life in it.

Moving on to verses nine and ten reminds us of our responsibility to the body. *"Then said he unto me, Prophesy unto the wind, prophesy, son of man, and say to the wind, Thus saith the Lord GOD; Come from the four winds, O breath, and breathe upon these slain, that they may live. So I prophesied as he commanded me, and the breath came into them, and they lived, and stood up upon their feet, an exceeding great army."*

The Father is still compelling us today to prophesy to His body. We are created in His image. He spoke the world into existence. He wants us to speak, as He commands, into our own lives and the life of His church. He is calling for the North, South, East, and West to come together in unison and speak life into His body. When we are in one mind and one accord the Holy Spirit will breathe new life into the body and it will stand an exceeding great army. It will stand for God and stand against the enemy. Jesus said *"I will build my church; and the gates of hell shall not prevail against it."* (Matt 16:18)

The Valley of Bones is about reconciliation. Our denominations have separated us, leaving us dry. We are consumed by religious spirits, having a form of Godliness, but without the power. Once we position ourselves to hear, we will be able to withstand more of His presence because we will have less of our own.

*Mattanah (present/offering)*

**Nahaliel** "Valley of God"
Peace in the midst of adversity

**Nahaliel** (Valley of God)

The only time this valley is mentioned in the Bible is in Numbers 21, our key text. It would appear we have little to draw from but there are some conclusions we can make. To start with, God is everywhere but His manifest presence is not. I tend to believe that He would frequent a location named "The Valley of God."

My next conclusion is derived from the order in which Nahaliel is mentioned in our key text. The premise that Israel's journey in Numbers 21 constitutes a picture of salvation, and their subsequent journey represents spiritual growth, is the foundation of this book. So we must consider the events before and after Nahaliel in the order of their occurrence. At Mattanah we presented ourselves as an offering unto the Lord. Bamoth, our next destination, means "high elevation." In between we have Nahaliel, the Valley of God.

As I've noted already the other valleys are in random order. We all go through them at different times according to

*Nahaliel The Valley of God*

God's discretion. I selected the valleys in between the various levels of growth, for this book, based on what I felt was pertinent to the plateau we were striving for. This valley was placed in the scripture by Divine inspiration. I believe the purpose for that lies with preparation. We cannot grasp the concept of resting while we "strive" until we have successfully negotiated the other valleys.

Nahaliel appears to be a microcosm of the growth process. We reach one plateau, experience new trials, and then God elevates us to the next level. The difference is how we respond in this particular valley. It is a valley and therefore a trial of some sort. Yet because God's presence is so near to us the trial seems insignificant. We are at rest during the trial. It is like finding out your old car has finally bit the dust but you have a check in your mailbox for a million dollars. God's presence puts things in perspective.

Most of us prefer to be on the mountain tops spiritually but the valleys are where you grow. If we must go through them, then why not have some peace, some rest, while we do so? Therein lies the objective of this valley; learn to go through the valleys and remain in perfect peace. *"Thou wilt keep him in perfect peace, whose mind is stayed on thee: because he trusteth in thee."* (Isaiah 26:3)

According to Hebrews Chapter 4, there is a place of rest that we can enter into. Let's begin with the first three verses. *"Let us therefore fear, lest, a promise being left us of entering into his rest, any of you should seem to come short of it. For unto us was the gospel preached, as well as unto them: but the word preached did not profit them, not being mixed with faith in them that heard it. For we which have believed do enter into rest, as he said, As I have sworn in my wrath, if they shall enter into my rest: although the works were finished from the foundation of the world."*

*Mattanah (present/offering)*

The rest referred to here is not Heaven. Canaan, the land flowing with milk and honey, is a shadow or type of rest. Joshua and Caleb were the only two of the original group leaving Egypt that were allowed to enter. Israel, upon entering into "rest," had to war against the inhabitants. There is no enemy in Heaven to fight, so Canaan is not a picture of Heaven.

Now let's examine these verses a little closer. The word "fear" in Hebrews 4:1 is referring to reverential awe. *"For God hath not given us the spirit of fear; but of power, and of love, and of a sound mind."* (2Timothy 1:7) Reverencing God is essential to our faith. Proverbs 1:7 *says "The fear of the LORD is the beginning of knowledge: but fools despise wisdom and instruction."* Joshua and Caleb trusted God. They had faith in His promise of a land flowing with milk and honey. The other ten spies were foolish and delivered a report based on fear, not of God, but of the inhabitants. Due to their faith, Joshua and Caleb were allowed to enter into the Promised Land along with a whole new generation.

Joshua and Caleb heard the word of the Lord and had faith that He was able to perform it. The writer of Hebrews is establishing the same principle here; entering into the rest of God is by grace through faith. We receive salvation, deliverance, healing, prosperity, and every other promise of God by the same means, by grace through faith. Every believer has a right to enter into His rest but many choose not to. The reasons vary: complacency, deception, ignorance, etc. For some it is fear. Not the reverential awe kind of fear, but rather the perverted "I'm scared" version. Some are scared to try, others are scared to fail, and many are scared of everything. Fear is the opposite of faith and it is of the enemy. To enter into rest you must lose your fear.

*Nahaliel The Valley of God*

Jesus said *"And these signs shall follow them that believe; In my name shall they cast out devils; they shall speak with new tongues; They shall take up serpents; and if they drink any deadly thing, it shall not hurt them; they shall lay hands on the sick, and they shall recover."* (Mark 16:17, 18) It is not enough to believe that God exists; we must believe that these signs will follow us. We must believe that we can enter in, we can take the land, and we can rest in the valley with His presence.

The Word must be mixed with faith, not fear. If we cannot believe that we can lay hands on the sick and see them recover then we are wasting our time and creating doubt for the person whom we're praying for. If you don't believe you can cast out devils then I highly recommend not trying. You may end up like the seven sons of Sceva in Acts 19 who attempted to cast out a demon only to be attacked by it. We must not only believe God and His Word, we must believe He wants to manifest His Word through us. Hebrews Chapter 4 is exhorting us to believe we have the right to enter His rest. He created it for us in the beginning. Don't fall short of the promise, mix the Word that you are believing for with faith and it will profit you.

Faith is what separated Joshua and Caleb from the rest of Israel. They believed the promise of God more than what they could see with their physical eyes. Exodus 33:11 makes it obvious that Joshua enjoyed the Lords' presence. *"And the LORD spake unto Moses face to face, as a man speaketh unto his friend. And he turned again into the camp: but his servant **Joshua, the son of Nun, a young man, departed not out of the tabernacle.**"* Caleb also differed from the rest of Israel according to Numbers 14:24, *"But my servant Caleb, because he had another spirit with him, and hath followed*

*Mattanah (present/offering)*

*me fully, him will I bring into the land whereinto he went; and his seed shall possess it."*

Let's move on to Hebrews 4:9-11. *"There remaineth therefore a rest to the people of God. For he that is entered into his rest, he also hath ceased from his own works, as God did from his. Let us labour therefore to enter into that rest, lest any man fall after the same example of unbelief."* There is rest in Nahaliel. Notice the criteria, faith and ceasing from our own works.

Growth is all about dying to the flesh so that there is less of us and more of Him. As long as we continue to do things our own way, God will not work through us to the extent He would like. *"But he giveth more grace. Wherefore he saith, God resisteth the proud, but giveth grace unto the humble."* (James 4:6) Remember, grace is God's influence working in your heart to manifest Himself in your life. If we are to retain the spirit of Caleb then we need to develop the practice of Joshua, fellowship. Resting is trusting God in the valley regardless of how it looks.

Twenty-three years ago I was contemplating quitting my job and relocating in order to be closer to my family. I didn't really like my job, my nearest relative was 400 miles away, and the woman I was interested in marrying only wanted to be friends. Not the ideal situation, but I prayed about it for a few days until I got a breakthrough. I was lying in a friend of mines' tanning bed and I asked the Lord what He wanted me to do in this situation. He said very clearly, "quit worrying, she is going to marry you." To which I replied, "Lord is that really you, or just wishful thinking on my part?" The Lord repeated Himself, "quit worrying, she is going to marry you," only this time He spoke a little louder. I wasn't convinced so I asked again, "Lord is that really you, I have to know?" The Lord then did something He had never done before or since,

He yelled ""quit worrying, she is going to marry you!" Three months later my wife and I were married.

Recently I started a new job in the same city most of my immediate family resides. My wife and I found a house we were interested in purchasing and she asked me to pray about it. I did and I heard the Lord say, "This is the one for now. Buy it and fix it up. When the market revives and you have some equity in it you can sell it and use the profit to help build the house you really want." Folks, I can't even think as fast as the Lord dropped that in my spirit, yet I had this twinge of doubt. So I asked, "Lord is that you, or my own thinking?" To which He promptly replied "Do I have to yell?" He had never brought the "yelling" incident of the tanning bed to my attention before so I knew I had heard from the Lord.

By now you're thinking that's an interesting story but what does it have to do with resting in God's Word? We found out later the house had already been sold. My wife was concerned, not that we didn't get the house, but that I had missed God somehow. She depends on me to hear from God. I told her not to worry, it wasn't over. Perhaps the buyer would back out, which he did. We're in the process of closing now. My point is that when you hear from God, you can rest in His Word.

I confess to you that I don't meet every trial I face with this type of rest. To go through the valleys with His presence, consistently, takes practice. What a difference it makes though! When you can maintain your joy, remain at peace, and speak faith filled words in spite of the circumstances, you will experience Nahaliel. It is not something you can "work up" by hoping or wishing. It is knowing in your inner man that God is on the throne. He loves you. He has a plan and a purpose for your life and He is going to take care of you and

*Mattanah (present/offering)*

your circumstances. So rest and enjoy your life now, where you're at, on the way to where you are going.

Verse 11 makes an interesting statement *"Let us labour therefore to enter into that rest."* In the Greek the definition of labour is "to use speed, be diligent, and to make an effort." The idea is that we must **want** the rest He is speaking of; we must have a desire to enter in. Nahaliel is near the end of our process for good reason. It is our experience in the other valleys that have taught us to rely on God instead of ourselves. The journey has been a process to build our faith to the point that we can trust Him instead of exercising our own wisdom.

Pisgah is where you are going but we have one more stop, Bamoth. Afterwards, there are just two more valleys before we reach our final destination. Your journey is nearly complete. I trust you are ready to move on.

# Chapter 8

## BAMOTH "High Elevation"

# CHAPTER 8

# Bamoth "High Elevation"

Alas, the mountain top. This is where we all long to be. Everything seems to be in order. We're healthy, our bills are paid, our relationships are well, etc. We have traversed enough valleys for a while. We are content to enjoy a time of rest. The devil doesn't appear to be anywhere in sight. All is well.

That's when something or someone comes along and reminds us of the law of gravity; what goes up must come down. I don't wish to discourage anyone but the truth is, while we are in the growing stage, we will spend a lot of time in the valleys. Growth comes via the valleys. Enjoy your time of rest during the mountain top experiences, but beware of complacency. It is easy to become too relaxed when everything seems to be going our way.

Mountains can be precarious. If you take a wrong turn you may find yourself at the edge of a cliff. There are jagged rocks, so watch your step. The scenery can be breathtaking, but don't allow it to become a distraction. We must be alert to watch and listen. The enemy is always lurking, waiting for an opportunistic time to strike. Sure, we have grown a lot to arrive at this level, but that doesn't mean we're immune to enemy attacks. In fact we will attract more opposition than ever before.

Please don't misunderstand me. The mountain is a good place to be. The higher the elevation, the farther we can see. This allows us to put things in perspective. The more mature we become, the greater our spiritual vision. We learn to mimic the eagle, which recognizes a storm is coming, and uses the proceeding winds to rise above it. But if we become complacent or distracted we will fail to discern the enemies approach. Remember to watch while you're drinking it all in, as did Gideon's' 300 chosen warriors.

## BE RESPONSIBLE!

When we are on the mountain, our faith is strong, as well as our anointing. Just remember, with anointing comes responsibility. Christ dwells in us through the Holy Spirit for a purpose. It's not about us, it's for His glory. He wants us to bring others to the Father, and edify those who are already believers. Evangelism and discipleship are two of the primary responsibilities to our fellow man.

Responsibility is becoming a lost art in today's world. We allow TV and video games to raise our children. We delegate to the government what we, as the church, should be doing. But most importantly, we have shunned our responsibility to God; As Paul said in Romans 12:1 *"which is our reasonable service."* Our reasonable service, according to Paul, was to present ourselves as a living sacrifice. In other words, God's will, not ours, be done. Learning to serve others at the cost of our own agenda is an art we all need to develop. While at Bamoth we should be in a good position to hear. Be obedient; be responsible for what you hear. Allowing God to govern your life will make you a friend of God, like Abraham. William Penn said "where God does not govern, tyrants will rule." Let God govern your life through the Holy Spirit.

Balaam is the ideal subject to illustrate the responsibility associated with anointing. I mentioned Balaam in chapter 1 as one of the "spots" recognized in 2Peter 2, and again in the book of Jude. Balaam has been dead for thousands of years, yet the spirit that drove him lives on vicariously through many "Christians" today. Some are unwitting accomplices; nevertheless they mar the Kingdom of God.

Balaam had a gift but chose to misuse it as many of us do today. He was the equivalent of a mercenary, a prophet for hire. He operated a harlot ministry, paid for by the highest bidder. Jesus said *"you can't serve God and mammon."* (Matt 6:24) Mammon represents the material things of the world, it's an idol. If we desire to grow in our relationship with the Lord, we must want Him more than we want "stuff." When Joshua told the people *"choose you this day whom ye will serve,"* he did so in reference to Balaam. *"Then Balak the son of Zippor, king of Moab, arose and warred against Israel, and sent and called Balaam the son of Beor to curse you: But I would not hearken unto Balaam; therefore he blessed you still: so I delivered you out of his hand."* (Josh 24:9, 10) Joshua went on to cite several other occasions the Lord delivered Israel before putting forth a challenge. *"Now therefore fear the LORD, and serve him in sincerity and in truth: and put away the gods which your fathers served on the other side of the flood, and in Egypt; and serve ye the LORD. And if it seem evil unto you to serve the LORD, choose you this day whom ye will serve; whether the gods which your fathers served that were on the other side of the flood, or the gods of the Amorites, in whose land ye dwell: but as for me and my house, we will serve the LORD."* (Josh 24:14, 15)

We all have that same choice and we have to make that choice every day, if not several times a day. We each have gifts designed to edify the body. How will you choose to use your gift(s) today? Will you serve God with your gifts or choose mammon? Jesus brings forth some perspective on the subject in Mark 8:36 *"For what shall it profit a man, if he shall gain the whole world, and lose his own soul?"* The Balaam spirit is counterproductive to the Kingdom of God. It is a "spot" that must be removed from God's people and the church. Never use your gifts selfishly or for monetary gain as your motive. Lay up treasures in Heaven, eternal rewards, instead of temporal gain.

Why is this relative, you ask, we are discussing the mountain top? I stated earlier that the mountain can be a precarious place. Balaam came to Bamoth with the hope of using his gift for gain. God had instructed Balaam not to come, and even used a donkey to warn him. Jesus said *"And whosoever shall exalt himself shall be abased; and he that shall humble himself shall be exalted."* (Matt 23:12) Balaam attempted to exalt himself. Experiencing Bamoth is like being on an extended "spiritual high." The danger is pride. Have you ever been in that place where you feel as if everyone else is at least one step behind spiritually? You have just exalted yourself and the fall is coming.

The Kingdom of God is supernatural. It doesn't operate naturally, it supersedes it. The word super means "above." While the supernatural is superior to the natural, it operates totally different. In the natural if we want to go up, we ascend by some means. But the way up in the Kingdom of God is down. We must remain humble. *"Pride goeth before destruction, and an haughty spirit before a fall."* (Prov 16:18) The original sin was pride, it was satans downfall. Don't allow it to be yours. Remember you are able to see better at this level. Don't let what you see sway you to become judgmental and self-righteous.

Let's examine the four most common pitfalls of the mountain top experience. I have already mentioned scenery, cliffs, and jagged rocks. The fourth I like to call PCS, Post Climatic Syndrome. Any one of these factors can spoil your experience but when they come in combinations they are a recipe for disaster.

**Scenery:**

Being caught up in the splendor of your surroundings on the mountain top is like driving on a curvy road blindfolded. While we should enjoy our chance for spiritual bliss, we must never let our guard down. It is easy to bypass ministry opportunities when you are distracted. It is easy to become selfish because we don't want to allow others to bring us down. Yet, if that is your attitude, you can be sure you are on your way back down. If we fail to make ourselves available for His use while we are on the mountain, then we will find ourselves back in the valley so quick it will cause us to scratch our heads in bewilderment.

Several years ago I took a motorcycle trip up the east coast with my Pastor and another church member. We saw some breathtaking scenery along the way but none as memorable as Bar Harbor Maine. As we rounded up the mountain I wanted to stop at every single vantage point to take pictures. The water was a deep blue, the sky was perfect, there were several small islands of nothing but greenery, and a large, white cruise ship in the harbor. It was truly indescribable. I can understand why so many artists migrate to that vicinity. After taking pictures and staring in awe at God's creation for quite some time, I realized I couldn't stay there. I had to leave, but I knew I wanted to return, and when I did I wanted to bring my wife with me. I wanted to share the experience again with her and witness her reaction.

That's how we should feel about our spiritual mountains. We should have a desire to encourage others to join us instead of becoming self-absorbed. It is easy to become selfish on the mountain because you feel so close to God you don't want to leave. But that is precisely what Jesus did. He gave up the splendor of Heaven to come to earth, share the beauty of His Father's creation, and use it to illustrate the Kingdom of Heaven so that others might experience it, and His Father's love.

**Cliffs:**

Whenever we take our eyes off our vision we inevitably end up on the wrong trail. Peter took his eyes off of Jesus for a second and immediately began to sink. God has a purpose for the valleys and a purpose for the mountains. The mountain is not a place of rest per se, but rather an opportunity to refocus on our vision. We are able to see clearer and farther. It is a place to "recharge our batteries," revitalize, and restore our motivation. Our mission is to be conformed into the image of Jesus Christ. Taking our eyes off Him or our vision can leave us at the edge of the cliff. Learn to move where and when God moves. Listen for His direction. It is easy to fall through the trap door of "leaning to your own understanding." *"A man's heart deviseth his way: but the LORD directeth his steps."* (Prov 16:9)

**Jagged Rocks:**

Perhaps you are enjoying the scenery, you're on the correct path, and you are following the Lord's leading. You

*Bamoth "high Elevation"*

don't feel distracted but suddenly you feel a sharp pain. The enemy blindsided you because you failed to watch and pray. You might ask, how can you fail if you are being led of the Lord? I'm reminded of David when he asked the Lord about going to battle against the Philistines, "shall I go up?" (2Sam 5) The Lord said "go" and promised him victory in the valley of Rephaim ("giants"). The Bible says the enemy "came up yet again" to war with David; the enemy doesn't give up easily. David could have based his decision to engage the Philistines on his last word from the Lord but instead inquired of the Lord a second time. This time God said "thou shalt not go up," and proceeded to give David a different strategy. David could have become complacent by basing his actions on recent history and would have tripped in defeat. Another important question David asked was, "how shall I go?" Most of the time, even if we pray and ask God for direction, we only hear the "go" command. We often fail to ask other pertinent questions, like; when shall I go, how shall I go, who shall I include, etc.

Without staying in tune with the Holy Spirit we will become complacent. Complacency is a sneaky foe. We rarely see it coming until we feel the pain of separation. It's not like the separation you experience when you sin, accompanied by conviction. This separation is more like feeling blissful until you are suddenly reminded of the loved one that has gone away and you begin to miss them. I'm sure I've mentioned it previously, but God doesn't want us to rely on methods. We can't rely on yesterday's word. If we lose our focus on the Father it is relatively easy for the enemy to trip us up. Tripping on jagged rocks is no fun.

Rock is becoming increasingly popular in construction and landscaping. It can be both beautiful and decorative. There is nothing wrong with that in the natural. But Jesus told us to build our **foundation** on the rock, not decorate our lives with it. If we have adorned our lifestyle with everything Christian, but lost touch with our foundation, we have become complacent. It's like being instructed by God to go do some type of ministry work. You gather your Bible, put on your witness wear, and jump in your car with the "I love Jesus" bumper sticker, and rush off to do the Lord's work. You have your favorite gospel CD playing, you're praying for grace, what more can you do? You can watch the road ahead for one thing, because you just ran over some jagged rock and now you have a flat tire. Coming down from the mountain can be deflating, so watch and pray.

**Post Climatic Syndrome:**

PCS can be defined as "an emotional letdown during or just after an event in which you had high expectations." Every one experiences disappointment in the natural, but in this context I'm referring to the spiritual high that comes with the mountain, and the reality check that inevitably follows when you have to leave. Whenever the joy level anticipated from an event fails to satisfy your expectation, you're at risk of PCS. Or perhaps the event is over, now the concern is you have no immediate spiritual aspirations or goals to look forward to.

The first time I used the phrase, Post Climatic Syndrome, was after several members of my Sunday school class had returned from a mission trip to Romania. Some of them were spiritually exhausted. I realized this was partially due to physical factors such as time differences, fatigue, cultural adjustments, and so forth. But physical reasons were not the entire story. They had been on an intense journey, anointed of God, and witnessed God move in mysterious and miraculous ways.

*Bamoth "high Elevation"*

Now they had to adjust to their normal lives: work, pay bills, mow the yard, etc.

PCS, like the jagged rocks, cliffs, and the distraction of scenery, can be avoided. It is a set-up from the enemy. The joy of the Lord is your strength and the enemy wants to steal it. He wants to kill, steal, and destroy. To avoid PCS: rest properly, be diligent about your quiet time, and surround yourself with mature believers. You must make a quality decision not to allow the enemy to steal your joy. The Word says God can "*do exceeding abundantly above all that you ask or think.*" (Eph 3:20) So not only can God bring you back to the mountain, He can take you higher.

Are you ready to go higher? Pisgah, our final destination, is just ahead. But first we must experience two more valleys; Berachah, and Eschol. Berachah means "prosperity or blessing." Eschol means "bunches of fruit." Either one sounds pretty good to me. Perhaps these valleys will be a joy to enter like Nahaliel. In any case they can't be all bad because they lead to Pisgah, the manifest presence of God.

*Nahaliel The Valley of God*

**Valley of Eschol** (Bunch of Fruit)

> *"And the Lord spake unto Moses, saying, Send thou men that they may search the land of Canaan, which I give unto the children of Israel: of every tribe of their fathers shall you send a man, every one a ruler among them."* (Num 13:1, 2)

You are probably familiar with the story. Of the twelve spies only Joshua and Caleb came back with a positive report. It is interesting to note that Joshua means "deliverer," and Caleb's name means "attack." If Israel had attacked, God would have delivered the land into their hands. The portion that the spies reconnoitered was so embellished with fruit that they named it Eschol. All twelve agreed it was "a land flowing with milk and honey" but only two of the twelve had the faith that it could be taken.

There were giants in the land, which caused the other ten to report *"we were in our own sight as grasshoppers."*

*Bamoth "high Elevation"*

After all that Israel had witnessed God do, you would think they would believe Him able. Yet the congregation chose to murmur and complain once again. They cried all night and longed to return to Egypt. Moses and Aaron fell on their faces to pray while Joshua and Caleb attempted to encourage the disheartened Israelites. The congregation was at the point of stoning them and choosing a new leader to take them back to Egypt. God, to put it mildly, was displeased. If Moses hadn't intervened God would have destroyed Israel and started over.

God didn't require their ability, He simply wanted their availability. Eschol was a valley with much promise but, as with most things, there was a price to pay. Israel, like many of us today, was not ready to pay that price. The bottom line here was simply faith in His Word. If God says He will do something we should regard it as a done deal. If you read verse two again you will see God said "I *give* unto the children of Israel." If God gives us something our response should be to believe it and receive it. As we mature in Christ we should learn to trust His Word regardless of the circumstances.

Due to their unbelief, that generation of the Israelites, never entered into the Promised Land. They died in the wilderness, forty years of wandering, then death. That scenario doesn't appeal to me, what about you? When will a generation of radical believers rise up and dare to take God at His Word? I personally believe the remnant is alive today. I believe we are at the Jordan on the threshold of entering in. I also believe, since you have come this far, that your spirit is bearing witness. But for some the journey will end here.

*"Wherefore, said they, if we have found grace in thy sight, let this land be given unto thy servants for a possession, and bring us not over Jordan. And Moses said unto the children of Gad and to the children of Reuben, Shall your brethren go to war, and shall ye sit here? And wherefore discourage*

*Nahaliel The Valley of God*

*ye the heart of the children of Israel from going over into the land which the LORD hath given them? Thus did your fathers, when I sent them from Kadeshbarnea to see the land. For when they went up unto the valley of Eshcol, and saw the land, they discouraged the heart of the children of Israel, that they should not go into the land which the LORD had given them."* (Num 32:5-9)

Jordan means "descender" in the Hebrew. Its root means "to descend or go down." Spiritually speaking it represents death. The tribes of Reuben, Gad, and half the tribe of Manasseh wanted to stop short of the Promised Land. They were comfortable where they were at. Sound familiar? They didn't want to go over the Jordan. This is representative of all the believers today who choose to stop short of all that God desires for them. Salvation is a truly wonderful gift that Jesus provided for us at Calvary. However there is much more in the atonement than fire insurance. There is deliverance, healing, and prosperity to name a few. These are all benefits that God wants us to exercise and enjoy.

Many today suffer from ignorance and deception in these areas. They can believe for salvation but never experience the fullness of God. God has made the ultimate sacrifice, the death of His Son, so that we might have an abundant life now. Be free now. Walk in health now. And prosper so that we might have to give, now. We receive these benefits the same way we receive salvation, by grace through faith. I trust you haven't come this far to stop short now. Let's cross the Jordan, die to our flesh, and take the land!

If you have never watched the movie "Facing the Giants" I highly recommend it. It's the story of a high school football coach with a losing record, an unreliable automobile, and although he and his wife long for children, apparently he is impotent. Does he grow bitter or get better; He is facing a crisis of belief. He decides to do something radical. He begins to praise God in spite of his circumstances and teaches his team to do the same.

Revival takes place at the high school. An appreciative father of a newly born again team member gives him a new truck. Miraculously he and his wife conceive, and his team goes on an incredible winning streak. In the end they find themselves facing the defending state champions, the Giants. It's a typical David verses Goliath tale. You know the rest of that story. Yes, it's a movie. All our circumstances aren't going to be tidied up in ninety minutes, but God is able. We need to praise Him in the valley as well as on the mountain. Perhaps if we do we won't have to circle the same mountain for forty years…

Now let's bring Eschol down to a personal level. I've mentioned before that the land represents our heart. If we want to take it and become fruitful we have some giants that we will have to overcome. Don't be afraid of them and stop short of the Promised Land. Choose to leave your comfort zone and dare to believe God and His Word. It will mean death to your flesh but the rewards are so much greater. Paul said in Romans 8:18, 19 *"For I reckon that the sufferings of this present time are not worthy to be compared with the glory which shall be revealed in us. For the earnest expectation of the creature waiteth for the* **manifestation of the sons of God**.*"* (The remnant to mature)

The manifest sons and daughters of God will display a radical faith. They will believe the whole truth, the entire Word of God. Not the denominational condensed versions we have created over the years to cover our ineptitude as the body of Christ. We can no longer afford to pick and choose what we want to believe while people continue to be in bondage, suffer needlessly, and die to face the reality of a burning hell. Some are sincere in what they believe, they are just sincerely wrong. By repeating the same "pattern" as their fathers, they discourage many from crossing over the Jordan. Unfortunately with that choice comes another lap around the mountain and a lot more time in the wilderness.

To doubt your ability to take the land is to actually doubt God's ability to do it through you and in you. We are overcomers, we are more than conquerors, and we can do all things through Christ! Amen. Praise God for the victory that is in Christ Jesus. Be part of the remnant that God uses mightily during the end times. Die to your flesh, cross the Jordan, and you will stand in the manifest presence of God at Pisgah.

Are you ready to move on? Just one more valley and I'll tell you up front, it's not a bad one. So if you are ready to cross over Jordan, escape your comfort zone, and face a few giants, then let's move on. Think of Peter. When he got out of the boat to go to Jesus the other disciples were holding a seminar on why they couldn't walk on the water. Leave the naysayers behind. I honestly have no desire to ruffle anyone's religious feathers, but Jesus was a radical. We are supposed to be conformed to His image. To do so will take some radical faith. The remnant are those who will attain Pisgah. Experiencing the manifest presence of God will put everything else into perspective.

*Bamoth "high Elevation"*

**Valley of Berachah**
*"Prosperity, Blessing"*

**Valley of Berachah** (Prosperity or Blessing)

> *"It came to pass after this also, that the children of Moab, and the children of Ammon, and with them other beside the Ammonites, came against Jehoshaphat to battle. Then there came some that told Jehoshaphat, saying, There cometh a great multitude against thee from beyond the sea on this side Syria; and, behold, they be in Hazazontamar, which is Engedi. And Jehoshaphat feared, and set himself to seek the LORD, and proclaimed a fast throughout all Judah. And Judah gathered themselves together, to ask help of the LORD: even out of all the cities of Judah they came to seek the LORD."* (2Chron 20:1-4)

Often in life we are attacked by the "ites." There are the work-ites, relative-ites, bank-ites, sick-ites, and even

197

the religious-ites. Jehoshaphat, whose name means "God judged", reacted properly in this particular situation. Our first order of business when adversity comes is to pray. Some "ites" may require prayer and fasting to be defeated. In any case we should always seek the Lord's help as soon as possible. It is also a good idea to involve some fellow believers to assist you. The Bible is full of passages that promote unity and illustrate the power of agreement between believers. My favorite and perhaps the most well-known would be what Luke wrote in the book of Acts, chapter 2, verse one, concerning the day of Pentecost. *"And when the day of Pentecost was fully come, they were all with one accord in one place."* They got rid of some ites that day. There were 3,000 converts the first day the Holy Spirit showed up.

Notice *how* Jehoshaphat prayed. It is similar to the Lord's model prayer in Matthew and Luke. *"And Jehoshaphat stood in the congregation of Judah and Jerusalem, in the house of the LORD, before the new court, And said, O LORD God of our fathers, art not thou God in heaven? and rulest not thou over all the kingdoms of the heathen? and in thine hand is there not power and might, so that none is able to withstand thee? Art not thou our God, who didst drive out the inhabitants of this land before thy people Israel, and gavest it to the seed of Abraham thy friend for ever? And they dwelt therein, and have built thee a sanctuary therein for thy name, saying, If, when evil cometh upon us, as the sword, judgment, or pestilence, or famine, we stand before this house, and in thy presence, (for thy name is in this house,) and cry unto thee in our affliction, then thou wilt hear and help.*

> *And now, behold, the children of Ammon and Moab and mount Seir, whom thou wouldest not let Israel invade, when they came out of the*

*land of Egypt, but they turned from them, and destroyed them not; Behold, I say, how they reward us, to come to cast us out of thy possession, which thou hast given us to inherit. O our God, wilt thou not judge them? for we have no might against this great company that cometh against us; neither know we what to do: but our eyes are upon thee."* (2 Chron 20:5-12)

Jehoshaphat acknowledges God for who He is, what He has done, and for what He has promised. Then Jehoshaphat made his petition, confessed his own wickedness, and said *"our eyes are upon thee."* It is sad but our eyes are usually everywhere else but on Him until we are desperate. We try to do everything our own way, until we have nowhere else to turn, then we say "God where are you?" God should always be "plan A" not "plan B, or C, or...." God created us for His glory. He desires a relationship with us. He wants us to depend on Him, look to Him, and rely on Him. When we do, He is able to help us. "The battle belongs to the Lord" was David's warning to Goliath just before he slew the giant.

This principle is repeated in our text by a prophet of Judah in verse 15. *"Thus saith the LORD unto you, Be not afraid nor dismayed by reason of this great multitude; for the battle is not yours, but God's."* He went on to say in the next two verses *"*[16]*To morrow go ye down against them: behold, they come up by the cliff of Ziz; and ye shall find them at the end of the brook, before the wilderness of Jeruel.* [17]*Ye shall not need to fight in this battle: set yourselves, stand ye still, and see the salvation of the LORD with you, O Judah and Jerusalem: fear not, nor be dismayed; to morrow go out against them: for the LORD will be with you."*

Our part will always be determined by God. The primary factors that determine a battle with the enemy are our faith in **His** ability and our obedience to **His** instructions. God will give you a battle plan if you are willing to listen. Once we are sure we have heard from God we should immediately begin praising Him before the fight even begins. That's what Judah did according to verses 18 and 19. *"And Jehoshaphat bowed his head with his face to the ground: and all Judah and the inhabitants of Jerusalem fell before the LORD, worshipping the LORD, And the Levites, of the children of the Kohathites, and of the children of the Korhites, stood up to praise the LORD God of Israel with a loud voice on high."*

Praise has a manifold purpose. It strengthens our faith, confuses the enemy, and best of all, God inhabits the praise of His people. The next time the enemy comes at you, confuse him. Start praising God before the battle begins and he will soon flee. Notice what David said in the first two verses of Psalm 8. *"O LORD, our Lord, how excellent is thy name in all the earth! Who hast set thy glory above the heavens. Out of the mouth of babes and sucklings hast thou ordained strength because of thine enemies, that thou mightest still the enemy and the avenger."* Praise stills the enemy.

Praising God before the victory will ensure it. It is a powerful weapon and an agent you will need to employ when your circumstances appear to be overwhelming. *"Submit yourselves therefore to God. Resist the devil, and he will flee from you."* (James 4:7) The first step is to submit yourself to God. Turn the problem over to Him and ask for wisdom and direction. *"If any of you lack wisdom, let him ask of God, that giveth to all men liberally, and upbraideth not; and it shall be given him."* (James 1:8) Once you have a game plan you *resist* by being obedient to the directions God has given you. When we attempt to war with the enemy our own way we end up assisting him instead of resisting him because we fail to utilize our greatest weapon, God.

David was a man after God's own heart. His greatest attribute was praise. He wrote the majority of the Psalms recorded in the Bible, which are songs of praise. He was a talented musician, and it's no coincidence, a mighty warrior. In his youth he played the harp to drive the evil spirits away from Saul. Praise is an enemy repellant. Develop your praise ability and you will increase your "resist ability." You will also discover your trials are shorter in duration because the enemy can't stand to be around you. As I heard Joyce Meyer say "praise and be raised or complain and remain."

In the next few verses we find Judah continued to praise and was delivered. *"And they rose early in the morning, and went forth into the wilderness of Tekoa: and as they went forth, Jehoshaphat stood and said, Hear me, O Judah, and ye inhabitants of Jerusalem; Believe in the LORD your God, so shall ye be established; believe his prophets, so shall ye prosper. And when he had consulted with the people, he appointed singers unto the LORD, and that should praise the beauty of holiness, as they went out before the army, and to say, Praise the LORD; for his mercy endureth for ever. And when they began to sing and to praise, the LORD set ambushments against the children of Ammon, Moab, and mount Seir, which were come against Judah; and they were smitten."* (Chron 20:20-22)

In summary: pray, fast (if led), until you hear from God. Then begin praising Him and obey. The "ites" won't stand a chance against a believer who is standing on God's Word. And to strengthen your position further, enlist the aid of some like-minded believers.

The exciting aspect of this valley comes after the victory. This is the valley of blessing or prosperity. Any valley can become a blessing of some form but this one is financial. Look at verses 25 and 26. *"And when Jehoshaphat and his people came to take away the spoil of them, they found among them in abundance both riches with the dead bodies, and precious jewels, which they stripped off for themselves, more than they could carry away: and they were three days in gathering of the spoil, it was so much. And on the fourth day they assembled themselves in the valley of Berachah; for there they blessed the LORD: therefore the name of the same place was called, The valley of Berachah, unto this day."* Proverbs 13:22 tells us *"the wealth of the sinner is laid up for the just."*

The remnant of God will prosper in the end times regardless of the global market. The purpose of Berachah isn't to line our own pockets, however, it is to further the Gospel. We will be actively involved in Kingdom work and become conduits for other ministries as well.

So let's welcome Berachah. It is an exciting place. We get to praise the Lord, watch the "ites" destroy themselves in utter confusion, then confiscate all their goods to support Kingdom work. Best of all, we are one step closer to the manifest presence of God, Pisgah.

# Chapter 9

## PISGAH "Cleft"

### Where the presence of God manifests

## CHAPTER 9
# Pisgah "Cleft"

---

> *"And the LORD said unto Moses, I will do this thing also that thou hast spoken: for thou hast found grace in my sight, and I know thee by name. And he said, I beseech thee, shew me thy glory. And he said, I will make all my goodness pass before thee, and I will proclaim the name of the LORD before thee; and will be gracious to whom I will be gracious, and will shew mercy on whom I will shew mercy. And he said, Thou canst not see my face: for there shall no man see me, and live. And the LORD said, Behold, there is a place by me, and thou shalt stand upon a rock: And it shall come to pass, while my glory passeth by, that I will put thee in a clift of the rock, and will cover thee with my hand while I pass by: And I will take away mine hand, and thou shalt see my back parts: but my face shall not be seen."* (Ex 33:17-23)

Can you envision God putting you in a safe place and then covering you with His hand? Now that's what I call security. No demon in hell can touch you there. Imagine, if you can, the peace, the joy, and the love you would experience with such intimate contact with the Creator of the universe. Then as He removes His hand you witness the glory of the Almighty God passing by.

Can you dream of such a relationship? Is it too much to ask? *"God is no respecter of persons."* (Acts 10:34) He desires a relationship just like that with each and every one of His children. That is why we were created. Adam communed with God this way on a daily basis in the garden. His choice to sin cost mankind those rights, but the Father restored them later through Jesus Christ, His Son. We can enjoy this type of relationship today.

Jesus is represented in our key passage as "the Rock" in verses 21 and 22. Moses was safe in the cleft of the rock just as Noah was safe in the ark; and we are "safe" if we know Jesus as our personal Lord and Saviour. The Old Testament is filled with symbolism and many of them have to do with Jesus. The Father desires to put us in a safe place and commune with us awhile. It is important to realize that we can't stay there indefinitely while we are still here on the earth. To do so would remove us from accomplishing His purpose for our lives. It would be like going to church one Sunday and enjoying it so much you didn't want to leave. But if you never left how could you fulfill the great commission? So we must take advantage of the opportunity to be encouraged by our Heavenly Father, then return to the rigors of everyday life, but with more of His presence manifest in our lives.

According to verse 17 Moses had found grace in the eyes of God. We find our grace in Jesus Christ. He is the only way to get to our "place," (verse 21) alongside God the Father. Jesus is, and has always been, the key to a God encounter involving the Father. John 1:1-3 tells *us "In the beginning was the Word, and the Word was with God, and the Word was God. The same was in the beginning with God. All things were made by him; and without him was not any thing made that was made."* Jesus also provided the "bridge" that spans the gap between us and the Father.

In John chapter 6, verse 28, the people ask Jesus *"What shall we do, that we might work the works of God?"* Jesus answered in the following verse *"This is the work of God, that ye believe on him whom he hath sent."* A relationship with the Father is impossible without first establishing one with the Son. Jesus went on to say later in John 14:6 *"I am the way, the truth, and the life: no man cometh unto the Father, but by me."*

Do you long to experience the manifest presence of God? Then you must; stand on the Rock, believe that you can, and find grace in the Father's eyes. Remember, we receive everything from God the same way, by grace through faith. God's grace is in us. If we have been saved we have faith. God's grace will manifest when we exercise the faith we have in His Son, Jesus Christ. So what is the problem?

The most notable deterrents from experiencing more of the presence of God are doubt and ignorance. James 1:8 tells us *"A double minded man is unstable in all his ways."* Verse 7 says *"For let not that man think that he shall receive any thing of the Lord."* We really don't need more faith, we need less doubt. As far as ignorance goes, consider Hosea 4:6 *"My people are destroyed for lack of knowledge: because thou hast rejected knowledge, I will also reject thee, that thou shalt be no priest to me."* God has made knowledge available. We have more preachers, teachers, books, tapes, and seminaries then at any other time in history. We have no excuse as far as resources are concerned. It all boils down to the "doing." Not only do we need to put feet to our prayers, we need to do it God's way. God is a God of order, but try not to think of it as rules and regulations. It's a process, not a law.

Let me remind you of the proper procedure for entering into the tabernacle. It is here that the body of Christ seems to be lacking. If we choose to be willfully ignorant of the proper process, God said in Hosea 4:6 *"because thou hast rejected knowledge, I will also reject thee, that thou shalt be no priest to me."* We all have a right to enter into the Holy of Holies, but God is a God of order. We are a *"chosen generation, a royal priesthood, an holy nation, a peculiar people"* according to 1Peter 2:9. But not everyone will choose to enter in because of fear, ignorance, complacency, or unbelief. I'm not saying these people are unsaved. I am saying they will never realize their full potential in Christ, nor be a part of the remnant.

The first step to entering the tabernacle involves death to the flesh. We must embrace the altar of sacrifice. God is not asking you to be a martyr, He desires a living sacrifice. *"I beseech you therefore, brethren, by the mercies of God, that ye present your bodies a living sacrifice, holy, acceptable unto God, which is your reasonable service."* (Rom 12:1) There are three distinctions in the Greek for the word *service* when translated. The one used in this passage is *"Latreia"* which means "ministration or worship of God." If you want to enter the Holy of Holies you must lay down your agenda, your desires, and approach God with an attitude of worship.

Next we come to the laver. This represents purifying ourselves through the washing of water by the Word. Romans 12:2 says it like this, *"And be not conformed to this world: but be ye transformed by the renewing of your mind, that ye may prove what is that good, and acceptable, and perfect will of God."* His ways are not our ways and his thoughts are higher than our thoughts. The mind of Christ is far superior to human intellect. The only way to develop that mind is through the study and application of the Word of God. The process, (valleys) provide opportunity to experience the Truth revealed to

*Pisgah "cleft"*

us by the Word. Remember, Jesus is "The Way, The Truth, and The Life." Jesus is The Word. To know Jesus, we must know the Word.

After the laver came the candlestick, the shewbread, and the altar of incense. The candlestick was to burn continuously. It was the priests' duty to keep the oil replenished so there was a constant light. Today we are the priests. It is our responsibility to maintain our oil, (Holy Spirit), so that we can be the light of the world. *"Ye are the light of the world. A city that is set on an hill cannot be hid. Neither do men light a candle, and put it under a bushel, but on a candlestick; and it giveth light unto all that are in the house. Let your light so shine before men, that they may see your good works, and glorify your Father which is in heaven."* (Matt 5:14-16)

Throughout the Bible bread is symbolic of the Word of God. Jesus Himself said, *"I am that bread of life."* (Jn 6:48) The shewbread was fresh daily. We need a fresh Word from God daily as well. You can only live on yesterdays' supper for so long. To remain healthy you need a steady diet consisting of the proper nutrition. It is vital we consume the Word on a regular basis. There are plenty of junk foods and desserts available, and they're not all bad; but Paul said in Hebrews 5 that "strong meat" belongs to mature Christians. "Strong meat" has to do with things associated with the Kingdom of God, starting with righteousness, peace, and joy.

Next is the altar of incense which, like the candlestick, was to burn 24/7. According to Bible symbolism and the reference in Revelation 8:3, 4, Incense represents the prayers of the saints. Paul exhorts us to "pray without ceasing" in 1Thessalonians 5:17. To the natural mind this would seem impossible, but to the spiritually minded person we know we can do all things through Christ. Prayer is communicating. You don't always have to be talking in order to communicate.

God is interested in your needs as well as those you may be interceding for, but He is more interested in simply communing. You cannot walk with the Lord in an intimate relationship without communication.

Finally we come to the veil. It was God's grace, Jesus Christ who rent the veil from top to bottom. We obtained the right to enter in, but we seldom exercise that right. To experience Pisgah we must obtain the favor of the Lord as Moses did. How can we do that? Everything from God is by grace through faith; just add obedience if you want favor and anointing. *"He that hath my commandments and keepeth them, he it is that loveth Me: and he that loveth Me shall be loved of My Father, and I will love him and will <u>manifest</u> Myself to him."* (Jn 14:21)

In summary to enter the Holy of Holies: 1) die to your flesh 2) assimilate the Word; head knowledge is a starting point, but experiential wisdom is the end result of practical application 3) maintain your walk through the guidance of the Holy Spirit 4) and seek the Lord constantly in prayer with an attitude of praise and worship.

## My Personal Experience in Pisgah

My first God encounter was like that of most believers, at the point of salvation. But unlike most believers my salvation experience was quite dramatic. I wasn't in a church; there was no sermon, a preacher, or anyone there to lead me to the Lord. God knows what it takes to get our attention and He got mine in a spectacular fashion. I want to emphasize that you don't have to be in a position of desperation in order to get saved, but I was.

I had just returned from a court appearance in which I was sentenced to 10 years in the penitentiary. I was overwhelmed with grief. I had one week to "get my life in order" before turning myself in to the penal system. I was 26 years old and my life had never been in order, so I don't know how I was supposed to rectify all that in seven days. I was desperate. I couldn't imagine surviving, for any length of time, in a small cage; without freedom, companionship, or the things we take comfort in and take for granted every day.

I was lying on the floor of my mother's den contemplating my choices and wondering how in the world I had arrived at this point. My best option seemed to be suicide. I just couldn't wrap my head around living in prison or the life I might face afterward. I was hopeless. My mind was searching for something, some reason, some ray of hope to cling to. I had always believed in God but why would He want to help me. I had never done anything for Him, but what did I have to lose.

I prayed a very simple prayer, "God, if you're real, show me." And He did, although in no way, shape, form, or fashion in which I was expecting. It was dark in the room but as I opened my eyes I saw a peculiar little light towards my right on the ceiling. At first I dismissed it as one of those spots that appear in your eyes after going from light to darkness. I couldn't ignore it, this was different. It wasn't going away, instead it was growing. It was taking on a form, a human form, but like a ghost.

I've shared my testimony many times over the years and I realize how dubious it may sound to others, but this was real. I can only report it as it happened. I had fought all my life, had guns aimed at my head, been shot at, jumped out of aircraft, repelled head first off cliffs, and faced numerous other precarious situations, yet without fear. I was so miserable I hadn't cared if I lived or died, so what was there to fear. But at that particular moment I was introduced to fear. I didn't recognize it initially, but my heart began to race, and I experienced for the first time the paralysis that accompanies fear.

The apparition was coming, slowly, towards me. It was solid white but I could distinguish a hood over its' head, the robe, and its' hands protruding from the sleeves. As it approached it began to stretch out its' arms and speak to me. It wasn't audible, nevertheless, very clear, "just take my hands and everything will be alright." So this must be Jesus coming to get me. God was answering my prayer, or so I thought.

I accepted my fate, this was it, I was going to die. It seemed better than the alternative so I started to reach out. My hands were inches from the apparition when I realized it had no face. Something was wrong with this picture. This wasn't Jesus. This must be the death angel, or some type of demon. My adrenaline was flowing, my heart and mind were racing as I realized I was going to die and go to hell. The events to this point had transpired in just a few seconds but it seemed like hours. Everything was so clear, God had answered my prayer. He showed me Heaven was a reality by showing me hell was real, and I was on my way.

I'm convinced, if they had investigated the cause of my death, they would have determined it to be a heart attack. In reality I literally would have been scared to death. One of my favorite scriptures is 1 Corinthians 10:*13 "There hath no temptation taken you but such as is common to man: but God is faithful, who will not suffer you to be tempted above that ye are able; but will with the temptation also make a way to escape, that ye may be able to bear it."* Even though I was lost at the time, God was merciful. He gave me a means of escape.

I snatched my hands away from the spirit before me, leapt to my feet, turned the light on, and dropped to my knees.

*Pisgah "cleft"*

Without a soul to witness it, a preacher, church, or an altar, I asked the Lord to save me and He did. I've heard many people over the years question their salvation, I never have. My first experience with God wasn't what I expected but it was real. I've never looked back and wished for something different because that was what it took for me to realize my need. I have never regretted my response to His unusual invitation.

My next God encounter came about two weeks later. I was in an old building with over a hundred other inmates waiting to be assigned a cell. It was a large open room with a petition dividing it into halves. There were 100 beds in each half, lockers, and a common bath with showers in the middle. It was loud during the day. Some of the men played cards while others talked loudly to overcome the blaring music that permeated the building. It wasn't exactly an ideal setting for reading or contemplation. Nevertheless, that is what I was attempting to do.

Someone had told me I should start reading the New Testament first so I did. I had just read Matthew 6:14, 15 *"For if ye forgive men their trespasses, your heavenly Father will also forgive you: But if ye forgive not men their trespasses, neither will your Father forgive your trespasses."* I didn't know anything about the Bible but I knew immediately God wanted to convey something important to me through these scriptures. So amid the chaotic atmosphere I began to meditate on forgiveness.

Suddenly everything was quiet. It was as if I were in a bubble, shielded from outside influences. What happened next was totally unexpected; I had a vision. I wasn't asleep but it was like a dream. I was in a beautiful field with tall grass and flowers. The sky was deep blue with an occasional puffy cloud. There was a man walking towards me, seemingly in slow motion. As he drew near I recognized him as my father. My father had died when I was 10. He was an abusive, alcoholic, who repeatedly told me he was the devil, and I believed him. The morning my family woke me to tell me he had died, I had simply said, "That's all you woke me for," and went back to bed.

Now here we were face to face having a civil conversation. He began to apologize and explain to me what had happened to him and how he had become the person he was. Once I heard his side of the story I was able to have compassion for him and truly forgive him. Until that moment I had never realized how much anger I had been carrying around. It was as though a giant burden had been lifted. It was nearly as powerful as my salvation experience. No sermon on forgiveness has ever impacted me as deeply as the vision I experienced that day.

You may not have a problem with forgiveness, perhaps your "giant" is something different altogether. Whatever it is, God wants you to defeat the bondage as soon as possible after you are saved. Otherwise, like in David's ordeal with Goliath's family, it will come back to haunt you later. Bondage will keep you from Pisgah. I had carried a chip on my shoulder my whole life and it had a name, unforgiveness. Bondage has fruit; mine was insecurity, anger, depression, etc. Don't allow the fruits of the flesh to hinder your relationship with God.

Over the next two years of incarceration I had several more God encounters. There were various ways He manifested His presence to me. God is everywhere but He chooses where, when, and to what degree He will manifest His presence. In a church service, for instance, He may show up ready to minister healing, or as your provider, or perhaps in a manner that allows you to experience His love.

*Pisgah "cleft"*

The event I want to share now illustrates His presence as a comforter and as a protector.

My cell mate had requested and received a transfer to a prison closer to his home in order to facilitate visits from his family. Another inmate had been assigned to my cell who was known as "Mad Jack." Jack was a Vietnam veteran and, to put it mildly, had anger issues. Jack had a reputation for forcing his cell mates to "check in." Check in was a term used for voluntary segregation. Anyone who felt their life was in danger could choose to do so. About the third day after he had moved in Jack warned me that I should check in before he returned from the yard. He didn't appreciate my Bible studies. I wasn't scared, yet I wanted to avoid a confrontation. I still didn't know much about the Bible but I didn't feel running away was the right thing to do.

Upon his return from recreation time in the yard it was obvious Jack was surprised I was still there and angry about it. He had been drinking and was in a foul mood. (Yes, there are drugs, alcohol, and even guns inside the prison walls.) I don't believe it was a coincidence that I was reading Psalm 37 at the time. Here are a few verses from that passage, *"¹Fret not thyself because of evildoers, neither be thou envious against the workers of iniquity. ²For they shall soon be cut down like the grass, and wither as the green herb. Rest in the LORD, and wait patiently for him: fret not thyself because of him who prospereth in his way, because of the man who bringeth wicked devices to pass. ⁸Cease from anger, and forsake wrath: fret not thyself in any wise to do evil. ⁹For evildoers shall be cut off: but those that wait upon the LORD, they shall inherit the earth."*

God gave me such strength in that situation. I informed him that I was neither going to fight nor was I going to flee. As he asked me if I was sure about that, he tilted his locker back enough to pull out something he had concealed there. When he turned around he showed me a "shank" and said if I didn't check in he would put his home-made knife through my heart that night.

One of the first scriptures I had ever memorized was Isaiah 26:3 *"Thou wilt keep him in perfect peace, whose mind is stayed on thee: because he trusteth in thee."* I had indescribable peace because I trusted the Word of the Lord more than the word of a convict. So I asked him if I could hold the knife. He was somewhat taken aback, nevertheless he handed it to me. It had an elongated oval handle that had roses engraved in it. The rose petals had been painted, as well as the greenery, and then coated with shellac. It was actually a piece of art. I asked him if he had made it himself, which he had, complimented him on his workmanship, and returned it to him. You could see the confusion on his face as I continued with my Bible studies. That night I slept as sound as ever.

The next morning after breakfast Jack left for the yard. I never saw him again. Apparently he tried his bullying tactics on the wrong person. He was sent to the "hole" (solitary confinement) for fighting and I was reclassified to minimum security before he was ever returned to population. I had forsook wrath, waited on the Lord, and inherited a much better situation.

The next God encounter I'd like to discuss has happened numerous times, and I hope you have experienced it as well. Its praise and worship time at church and someone executes a small act of obedience that ushers in the manifest presence of God. The manifestations differ, but ordinarily this becomes the service; no preaching is necessary. I demonstrated my corporate anointing theory earlier and this could be a factor in the scenario. The hunger level for His presence is also a key. In any case His grace will always be according to His mercy, His timing, and to the extent He desires. This type of God encounter isn't manufactured by man's efforts, it is His response to a simple act of obedience by an individual or the church as a whole.

I mentioned that to be a candidate for Arnon, (radical stream) God may impress you to do some strange things at times. Being obedient to those promptings can be very rewarding. God has impressed me to go pray for someone during praise and worship, or go to the altar without knowing why. These are hardly strange things, but they are acts of obedience that prompted someone else to act, then another, and another, until the entire church was moving in the Spirit.

Once during worship service I noticed my wife weeping, which wasn't that unusual, but suddenly, and loudly, she cried out. That must have been a contact point for the Spirit because it seemed as if her cry penetrated every heart present. We were weeping, shouting, repenting, hugging, praying, and rejoicing for the entire service. We still refer to it as "Georgie's cry." The simplest acts of obedience can cause a magnificent move of God.

God doesn't limit Himself to the confines of the church building. I've experienced amazing moves of God while ministering to others in jail, in their homes, or in the workplace. I've also been alone numerous times, praying, writing, or listening to praise and worship music when suddenly God shows up. God is looking for opportunities to manifest His presence. He longs to fellowship with His children. We need to desire His fellowship as much as He desires ours.

My typical reaction during a strong move of the Spirit is to cry. I become overwhelmed with gratitude. The Creator of the Universe is taking time to visit the small speck of dust we call Earth. He is allowing us to sense how awesome He is and how much He truly loves and cares for us. I feel so unworthy, yet I reject condemnation, instead I am inspired to do better. I trust you are as well.

This entire book is dedicated to inspire you to grow. From valley to valley, plateau to plateau, Oboth to Pisgah, we climb. As we climb we are transformed. Becoming more like Jesus is the single most important act that any of us can possibly endeavor to achieve. Jesus pointed everyone He came in contact with to the Father. It must be our objective as well. In order to do so effectively we must **demonstrate** the Kingdom of God like Jesus did so that we can **proclamate.**

I'm sure you realize that reading this book through did not instantly mature you, nor suddenly bring you into the manifest presence of God. It is a process, and it takes time. Don't lose hope. John 8:31 says *"Then said Jesus to those Jews which believed on him, if ye continue in my word, then are ye my disciples indeed."* John 14:21 goes on to say, *"He that hath my commandments, and keepeth them, he it is that loveth me: and he that loveth me shall be loved of my Father, and I will love him, and will manifest myself to him."*

Growth, unfortunately, is not everyone's desire. Many will choose to just hang in there till Jesus comes. Do you want more? Do you want to be used in a powerful way in these last days? Is your desire to be one of the remnant God is raising up to demonstrate through before Jesus returns? Then begin to practice the principles necessary to promote you to the next level, whatever that level may be. Be an overcomer in the valleys! You **CAN** do all things through Christ which strengthens you! You **ARE** more than a conqueror through Him that loves you!

May God bless you and keep you as you endeavor to seek His presence, praise Him, and point others to Him. I trust that I will cross paths with you in the valleys. And soon,

*Pisgah "cleft"*

and very soon, we will meet on the battlefield where the remnant makes her final stand just prior to when Jesus makes His. Then I believe He will say once again, "It is finished.